Sibling Revelries

Finding Family After

Sixty-Two Years

Mary Jo Latham-Martin

Sprin

Publisher's Note:

Text Copyright © 2018 by Mary Jo Martin

Paperback ISBN: 978-0-692-07867-9

Cover Design – Dylan Drake
Cover Image – Shutterstock
Interior Formatting – Manon Lavoie

Imprint: Siblings Publishing

LCCN: 2018902509

Spring, Texas
10 9 8 7 6 5 4 3 2 1

Dedication

To my entire family—the Lathams and the Martins

Acknowledgements

I owe a huge debt of gratitude to my very patient and cooperative husband, son, daughter-in-law, and grandchildren for listening to my endless complaints and whining about how difficult this has been. And, for their joy at what I've accomplished.

Many, many thanks must go to my Houston Writers Guild Critique Circle. They listened for literally years while I struggled to transition from someone who wrote business documents to someone who can tell a story. Names must be named: Monica Stanton, our first fearless leader; Vanessa Porta, who took over as leader, and has a great story that's just waiting to be told; Regina Olsen, teller of tales of archangels, demons, and vampires; Clara Jane Sweet, purveyor of historic romance—as well as most excellent tales in other venues; Natasha Storfer, who takes us to unimaginable worlds in some of the most beautiful prose I've ever read; Steven Malone, who trusted me to proofread and edit several of his works, and taught me a lot about reconstruction following the Civil War in Texas; Ernie Garcia, writer supreme and ex-English teacher who caught me out on many bloopers, and whose stories just have to be published.

A great deal of credit must also go to writing coach Max Regan, who started me on the journey of transforming what began as the parents' stories into a memoir.

To Roger Leslie, who did a fantastic global edit; your skills and support have been invaluable.

Ron Bitto, with an MFA in Drama-Playwriting from Yale, who somehow wound up in the oil patch, was a fast and thorough beta reader.

Myra Jolivet, author of two Creole mysteries, was the culprit who started me on this adventure. She is a former client, and we got together after work one night over Martinis. After I told her my story, she said, "You have got to write this." It was an order; I had to do it.

Table of Contents

Part One

The Start of it All

*"You have to study a great
deal to know a little."*
CHARLES DE SECONDAT

Chapter One

Beginnings

"Sweet are the uses of adversity, which, like the toad,
ugly and venomous, wears yet a precious jewel in
his head; And this our life, exempt from public haunt,
finds tongues in trees, books in the running brooks,
sermons in stones, and good in every thing."
WILLIAM SHAKESPEARE

It started with a quiver in my voice, a shaky hand, and a worried heart. I first noticed it in 2003, when I was fifty-seven. That quiver in my voice and my shaky hand didn't fit well with my image as a self-confident, competent, take-charge professional. It also scared me. I began to imagine that it was due to some kind of horrible condition, from a brain tumor to Parkinson's disease. The more I worried, the worse it got.

I was working at a small business-to-business ad agency, running the Research and Database Marketing group. My job was to manage the efforts of this team, ensure the studies were done correctly and on time, then present the results to our clients. Being a left-brained, analytical, by-nature curious type, helping our clients solve their business challenges was a great deal of fun for me. After years of holding down marketing communications roles, I'd finally found my specialty, and I loved the work. Although their dilemmas might not have been as compelling as a good murder whodunit, we usually uncovered some surprises.

We also frequently unearthed some tidbits that could have major financial consequences, and it was wonderful to be able to tell clients how much money they could save or gain in additional revenues. We did a number of projects where clients had double-digit returns on the money they spent on research. That turned a research spend into an investment, something any decent businessperson could appreciate. Those were the best assignments we had, and they usually led to repeat business for us.

One of our most memorable projects involved a comercial feasibility test for an engineering firm. During the presentation of the results, the president of the client company jumped up, banged his fist on the table, and shouted, "Holy shit! I knew it!"

He was a large, florid man, who looked like he might have a bad temper, and I wasn't sure if he was pleased or planned to hit me. Fortunately, as it turned out, he was extremely pleased. His company of left-brained engineers had convinced him that a new idea they had would make them all rich and famous. Our research showed that interest in it among companies that might be likely to buy it was lukewarm at best. The results of the research saved his company at least a million dollars in development costs. That man was one happy client. This is the kind of experience market researchers live for.

His project and others provided extraordinary case histories when we prospected for new business, and we loved telling those stories. Although the work was a passion for me, I did not initially enjoy sharing the results with clients. Eventually, after years of practice, my skills improved, and those presentations even became somewhat pleasurable. Like many ad agencies, ours was a culture of being somewhat intimidated by our clients—since in their minds they were always right. Of course, they pay the bills. As someone with a less than robust dose of self-confidence, I fit into that culture easily, so it took some time for me to relax enough to enjoy what I did well. I liked the prospecting even less, until I learned to let the prospects talk first and then explain to them how we could help them. It was like telling a story. Then it became fun.

When presenting those research results, or meeting with prospective new clients, I gradually became aware that my voice was sounding different. It cracked and was slightly shaky. It resembled Katharine Hepburn's. If you're old enough, you'll remember her. She was a very famous actor with a career that began in the 1930s and lasted seven decades. I used to watch old movies late at night with my mom and grandmother when I was a kid on our twelve-inch black and white TV. *The African Queen*, staring Katharine and Humphrey Bogart, was one of our favorites. She, along with Lauren Bacall, were two of my idols. My goal was to grow up to be as sophisticated and glamorous as they were in those films from years gone by. Although Hepburn was one of my much-loved actors, I most certainly did *not* want to sound like her. Lauren Bacall, by comparison, sounded much better, with a deep, sultry voice. Unfortunately, I never had a sultry voice, and alas, I wound up sounding like Katharine did in her later years.

Katharine Hepburn (left) and Lauren Bacall (right).
What impressionable young girl wouldn't want to
be like either of these beauties? Images in the
public domain from Wikimedia Commons.

Around the same time, I noticed the vocal crack and hand shaking, I also perceived a change in my handwriting. It just didn't look as good as it had, with the letters appearing somewhat shaky. When I first started to write something, it was really bad; fortunately, it diminished a bit as I wrote more. When I signed my name, either on a check or a charge slip, the Ms (and I had two of them—Mary and Martin) would be particularly squiggly. I'd always written well in longhand, although it was not as beautiful as my mother's. She learned to write in the heyday of gorgeous penmanship.

As a kid in the 1950s, sitting at our little flip-top desks, we learned The Palmer Method for cursive writing. Woe unto you if you did not reproduce those letters correctly. Worse, if you were unlucky enough to go to Catholic school, the nuns would crack your knuckles with a ruler for that infraction. Kids now have no idea what cursive is, and even our teenaged grandchildren struggle with trying

Example of writing using The Palmer Method.
Image in the public domain from Wikipedia.

to write anything in longhand. It makes you wonder how their signatures for legal purposes will be handled in the future. Like hieroglyphics, our cursive writing will some-day be studied by archeologists attempting to understand our civilization.

Finally, I began to have problems holding drinking containers like coffee cups or glasses. When I attempted to hold something with one hand, a very obvious tremor would start. This was worse in my left hand, so whatever was in the glass or cup would spill. This is not good in business situations, when you're juggling a cup of coffee or an adult beverage in your left hand, keeping your right hand free to shake hands (in a good way) with clients or prospects.

People would see this and say, "Are you OK?"

I'd smile and say, "Of course. I've probably just had too much caffeine (or had a rough day, if I was holding a glass of wine)."

I found it horribly embarrassing. In addition, the more it was brought to my attention, or the more stressed I was, the worse it got. Since I was a kid, I never liked to draw attention to myself, particularly if I felt I was being different or weird in some way. Those tremors were most definitely different. The only people I'd seen with anything remotely resembling them were old people or people with something horrible like Parkinson's disease. I certainly did not consider myself old and hoped with all my heart that I did not have Parkinson's.

These symptoms worried me, and the more concerned I became, the worse they got. After putting it off and putting it off (I was a busy woman, after all), I mustered my courage and went to see my internist.

He began by saying he wasn't sure what it was. Although I was relieved he didn't tell me to get to an emergency room immediately, this wasn't what I wanted to hear. In fact, he seemed as puzzled as I was. Hearing uncertainty from an expert only served to make me more anxious than I'd already been. I was not exactly reassured. He went on to say it could be due to a lot of things, and suggested I visit a neurologist. That made me really nervous. In my mind, neurologists only dealt with big, serious brain problems. I panicked, thinking, *oh my God; do I have a brain tumor?* He didn't tell me what I wanted to hear, that it was nothing to worry about. My mystery remained unsolved and my anxiety reached a peak.

One of my co-workers at the ad agency had a brain tumor. I watched with dread as she struggled through cryo-knife surgery and wave after wave of follow-up radiation sessions. It was terrifying to watch and hear about. Although she came through it fine, I did not want to repeat her journey.

The neurologist I was referred to was able to see me fairly quickly, so I didn't have to stew on this for too long. Good thing, since my fears, and probably my blood pressure, were off the chart. Dr. Virgadamo turned out to be a terrific guy, kind, and with a great sense of humor. After examining me and asking some questions, he erased my distress and dread by giving me the best news a doctor probably could, under the circumstances.

"You don't have anything serious," he explained. "What you're living with is due to something called familial or essential tremor. It's caused by misfiring of the neurons in a specific area of the brain. No one really understands what causes it. It's easily treatable with medications that have been around for years. They're safe and effective, and best of all, they're cheap!"

He then went on to tell me there are a number of famous people who had this disease—notably, Katharine Hepburn. I finally understood why I was sounding like her.

Dr. Virgadamo asked, "Does it get better after you have a glass of wine, or some other alcoholic concoction?"

"As a matter of fact, it does," I replied, surprised.

He suggested, grinning, "Well then, you should have a glass of wine in social situations. Or any other time you want one."

I *really* liked this man. Not only had he defused my fear of a brain tumor, but his most excellent sense of humor and understanding of what I was going through were just what I needed.

He went on to explain more about the disease and then turned the diagnosis into a medical mystery. "No one truly understands why these neurons misfire, however, it *is* an inherited disease."

I blurted out my usual response of, "No one in my family ever had a problem like this!" Then, in a blinding flash of the obvious, it entered my thick head that I was totally ignorant about half of my genetic makeup.

The neurologist saw the shocked look on my face and asked, "Are you all right?"

I replied, "Yes, but it just occurred to me that I know nothing about my father's contribution to my genetics. I never knew him, and I don't know anything about him or his family."

For years, I'd been avoiding that issue. Not only in doctors' offices, when giving medical histories, but also in day-to-day life. I realized that if I were to get to the bottom of this familial tremor mystery, I'd have to start working on family history.

I was raised by a single mother, in a loving multi-generational household. We shared a home with her parents. Most of my life, I knew nothing of my father. I understood that he was in the service during World War II. I had a grainy old black and white photograph in my baby book which I cherished for years of a handsome man with dark, wavy hair, and what looked like beautiful sparkling light-colored eyes with a hint of mischief in them. He was wearing Navy dress blues, standing alone rigidly with his arms at his side, looking straight into the camera lens. He was almost at attention, in front of a US flag, trying to suppress a smile and look very serious. I can remember staring at it as a little girl, wishing that by studying it intently, I could somehow magically make him appear. I knew his name from my birth certificate, and that he was from Kentucky. That was the totality of my knowledge of this man who may have passed on a neurological disease to me. And heaven only knows what else.

As a child, when I'd ask my mother about him, she'd brush me off and say brusquely, "There's not much to know. He was killed in the war." I never believed her and wanted to know much more of their story. Despite my best efforts, she'd never say any more. By the tone of her voice, I knew not to prod her for any other information.

Even my husband, David, tried to get more information out of her. When we were dating, I distinctly remember him asking her, "So, what was Mary Jo's dad like?"

She snapped, "He was a son of a bitch, and the less we talk about him, the better."

Here I was, stuck fast in a predicament. How on earth could I uncover the family medical history of a man about whom I knew virtually nothing? By the time of my diagnosis, my mother and grandparents had passed away, and everyone else in my family knew less than I did, so I didn't have anyone to harass for more information.

After my diagnosis, I learned to cope with this condition, so I didn't immediately begin to search for my father or his family. During this time, I took what my neurologist called "baby doses" of the medications used to treat it and tried speech therapy for my quivering voice. Despite the annoyances this disease presented, I was eternally grateful that I didn't have something worse, like Parkinson's disease.

Speech therapy was an interesting and enjoyable experience. I had a business acquaintance who had a speech therapy practice. She wanted to get some feedback on a potential new product they were thinking about introducing. I had a shaky voice, but knew how to get her the input she needed to make a business decision. So, we made a trade. I got her data, and one of her speech therapists helped me to calm my shaky speaking somewhat. Jane and I had a series of weekly sessions, and I learned how to modulate the pitch of my voice slightly to get it to sound more like what I considered "normal." It was a win-win situation, and the therapist was a very kind and thoughtful person. Like my neurologist, she also had a great sense of humor, so our sessions were usually fun.

She'd get me talking about something (to assess how my therapy was progressing) and we'd end up laughing our heads off about some of my adventures in entrepreneur land.

Of all the neurological diseases, this was the least scary, even if it resulted in some unusual symptoms I had to learn to deal with. I could relate to the Little Mermaid who traded her voice for legs so she could be with the handsome man who discovered her. But I didn't get a gorgeous guy in exchange. Nevertheless, far worse things could have happened to me. The best news of all was that it wasn't a brain tumor.

Then TV and the National Geographic Society stepped in.

Chapter Two

The Deep Roots
How Humans Filled the World

"The wind makes you ache in some place that is deeper than your bones. It may be that it touches something old in the human soul, a chord of race memory that says migrate or die—migrate or die."
STEPHEN KING

In 2005, *The National Geographic Society*, in conjunction with IBM, launched the *Genographic Project*. They have been working on this mission for over ten years, using DNA analysis to track human history, migration, and our connections with one another. The results of this effort have helped archeologists, anthropologists, ethnographers, and a host of other scientists who spend their lives trying to understand our roots and how humanity spread across the globe. It has also provided countless hours of enjoyment to anyone who is interested in these topics. I was one of them.

I've harbored a hidden desire since I was a child to be either an archeologist or anthropologist, so knowing about this allowed me to live out this dream surreptitiously. I can vividly remember watching a program when I was a child that aired on one of our local TV stations called "What in the World." It was hosted by two archeol-ogists from the University of Pennsylvania. They'd show an artifact, then ask their guests what it was and what time period it came from. After watching for a while, I discovered that I came pretty close to guessing where some of those things had come from. It was my one and only archeology course.

The *Genographic* website describes the mission as "working with indigenous communities around the world to help answer fundamental questions about where humans originated and how we came to populate the Earth." They say that it was, and continues to be, "a study of human migration on a grand scale over a 60,000-year time span." Best of all, "a portion of the proceeds from sales of their *Genographic* kits funds further research and the *Genographic Legacy Fund*, which in turn supports community-led indigenous conservation and revitali-zation projects." So far, about 750,000 people in over 140 countries have participated in this endeavor.

A couple of years after I'd been diagnosed with familial tremor, a PBS documentary happened to air about the *Genographic* project. They explained what it was and showed how the ancestors of everyone in the world had originally come out of Africa and spread throughout the earth. One path went through the Middle East and into Europe and Central Asia, branching eventually into the Americas, either over the Russia to Alaska land bridge, or by sea. Another went through India and along various coastlines to the Far East, Southeast Asia, Australia, and Oceania.

My husband, David, and I were trained as chemists, and we have shared a lifetime of love for any kind of science.

Here's the migratory map for all of our roots from the Project's website:

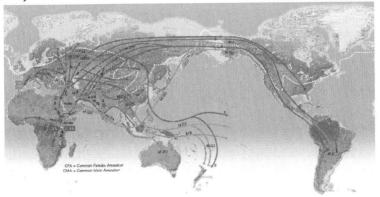

Human migratory paths out of Africa.
Permission to reproduce image from NGS/
National Geographic Creative.

While he stayed with it for his entire career, I later veered off in a different direction. This documentary was right up our alley. We were glued to the TV while the program aired. They explained how they were looking for as many people as possible to populate their worldwide genetic database. For a small amount of money, and a painless cheek swab to gather some cells, you could contribute your DNA and be part of a global adventure in anthropology and human migration.

Eventually, they set up a system designed to help connect people with similar DNA patterns. Although this is interesting, many of these people have not shared family names or family trees. While you may share some genetic relationship with them, they're essentially dead ends for finding family. Although some have shared a bit of information, these people have turned out to be very distant cousins of mine on my mother's side.

Disappointingly, none of them could be tied back to my father's family. That's because for women, this testing, unlike some we had done later, looked only into my mother's ancestry, using what is called mitochondrial DNA or mtDNA. Men learned their paternal ancestry through their yDNA, but nothing of their mother's contribution. Although I didn't know it at the time, I'd later discover a fascinating tie on my father's side through a different type of DNA testing from a company called *23andMe*, who examined both maternal and paternal contributions.

We were all over it. I told David, "You know we just *have* to do this, don't you?"

He responded, "Well, of course we do."

We sent for our kits, swabbed our cheeks, and waited excitedly for the results. Although what we learned about our distant ancestors was interesting from an academic standpoint, it wasn't terribly surprising. We were both fairly certain that our families had come out of Europe, and the maps we got that showed their migratory patterns were about what we expected. Nevertheless, they were thought-provoking, and helped to illustrate how humans have connected and migrated over thousands of years.

Here's what the project had to say about my ancient ancestry:

"The common direct maternal ancestor to all women alive today was born in East Africa around 180,000 years ago. Though not the only woman alive at the time, hers is the only line to survive into current generations.

From East Africa, groups containing this lineage spread across the entire African continent. Between 60,000 and 70,000 years ago, some groups moved from Africa to Asia. Your line traces to one of these groups.

Your ancestors first settled West Asia (now Armenia, Azerbaijan, Bahrain, Georgia, Iran, Iraq, Kuwait, Oman, Qatar, Saudi Arabia, Syria, UAE, and Yemen). From there, they expanded toward the Levant region. The Levant is now composed of Lebanon, Syria, Jordan, Israel, Palestine, Cyprus, Hatay Province, and other parts of southern Turkey, some regions of northwestern Iraq, and the Sinai Peninsula.

Following that they moved into Europe."

Beyond a geography lesson, I discovered I'm basically European, with an ancient dash of Middle Eastern and likely a smidgeon of Eastern European. I think this explains some of my food preferences—like a love for hummus and other Middle Eastern foods.

David's ancestry turned out to be similar, but with a side trip through the Balkans. Here's what they had to say about his ancestry:

"The common direct paternal ancestor of all men alive today was born in Africa around 140,000 years ago. He was neither the first human male nor the only male alive in his time. He was the only male whose direct lineage is present in current generations. Most men, including your direct paternal ancestors, trace their ancestry to one of this man's descendants.

Your branch of this lineage traveled with out-of-Africa migrants to Asia. From there, they journeyed west to the Balkans in southeastern Europe.

With the end of the last ice age, your ancestors helped resettle Europe."

Interesting that they've been able to trace women back significantly further than men. This was absolutely fascinating. While it gave us some insights into our far-distant forebears, it didn't tell us anything about our more recent ancestry. Obviously, it provided no clues on where I'd inherited my familial tremor. That had to come from much more recent history.

In a video on the National Geographic *Genographic* website to encourage people to participate in the project, they said, "By participating, you'll learn more about yourself than you ever thought possible."

I could certainly relate to that. They had no idea the path this would start me on and just how true this eventually would be for me.

Chapter Three

What about the Shallow Roots? Digging

"Truth, when not sought after, rarely comes to light"
OLIVER WENDELL HOLMES

After our *Genographic* journey, and learning about our ancient ancestry, my husband and I found ourselves wanting to know much more about our heritage.

As David put it, "That ancient DNA stuff is cool, but it only shows what happened tens of thousands of years ago. I'd like to know something more recent. And I know you would too."

I obviously wanted much more information, including details that might help explain my medical mystery, familial tremor. Specifically, whether it came from my father or from someone else in his family.

I was also driven by a thwarted lifelong desire to know more about that handsome man in the Navy dress uniform who was my father.

By the time David and I were sneaking up on retirement, both of us became interested in family histories. As you get older and your kids go out on their own, it frees you up for other pursuits. You have to fill that time that you used to spend with kids or grandkids with something. For David and me, it was the realization that it would be interesting to know more about our heritage. Passing those histories on to our son and his children, and so on down the generations would give us a sense of living on beyond our mortal years. Beyond that, our descendants might have medical mysteries too.

We started by discovering and subscribing to *Ancestry.com*. For a relatively modest subscription fee, their website allows you to build and grow your own family tree. It has millions of data points, including census data, immigration and military records, and church records for births, baptisms, marriages, and deaths. The data come primarily from the United States, but they are continuing to add more and more records from other countries. Ancestry keeps increasing the documentation you can access as a cadre of volunteers digitizes old records. There are also other people's family trees on the site, some of which are public and searchable. The web designers have cleverly developed a little leaf graphic, which may appear on someone in your tree. Their presence means that there is some sort of record on them other than the ones you have—either governmental data like census, military, and church records, or other members' trees.

Once you get your own tree started, you can frequently find other members' trees with your family in them. These sometimes show people further back in time than those in your tree, so with a click of your mouse, you can easily add ancestors that are more distant. Still, you have to be careful. If those ancestors aren't documented well, you're just taking someone else's word for it. We all know that just because it's on the internet, doesn't necessarily make it true. We've run into many instances of people's trees where fathers were born after their children, and other nonsensical information. Worst, there are some trees that have no documentation at all. We avoid those, since they probably indicate that people have simply copied from other people's trees without doing much work.

Unlike me, David comes from a large family. He is one of eight, with four brothers and three sisters. He also has a horde of nieces, nephews, and cousins. Most of his siblings are half-brothers and sisters, since his father was married three times. Understanding which of them were from which mother and keeping track of all of them was challenging at first. After all, I had a limited cast of only nine close family besides me—my mother, two grandparents, two uncles, two aunts, and two cousins.

Meeting David's family was a major culture shock for me as well. I grew up in a big city, while he is from a small coal-mining town of about 600. The strangeness I felt was both for the multitudes of people in his family, and for the environment.

For years, his relatives were the only big family I had. We lived in Philadelphia at the time, and many of them lived in Western Pennsylvania, so visiting was relatively simple. All it took was a five-hour ride on the Pennsylvania Turnpike. Of course, that's without stops, which is nearly impossible. After traversing some tunnels under the mountains, and up and down the beautiful hills of western Pennsylvania, I was plunged into their big clan. Interestingly, although they were David's half-siblings, it never felt like they were anything but full-blooded relatives.

David and I were both the only ones in our families at the time who had gone to college, so when we visited we were treated like royalty. We were the success stories. We got out. People living in that part of the state didn't have many job opportunities back when he was a child. That's changing now as the younger generations are growing up. We're very happy about that. Most men, back in the 1950s or earlier, went to work in the coal mines, which provided decent wages, but dangerous working conditions, with injuries and "black lung" disease common. Black lung is the common name for coal workers' pneumoconiosis, and it turns otherwise healthy pink lung tissue black from inhaling the coal dust. One of David's sisters was married to a coal miner, so we saw first-hand the toll it took on men's bodies.

———————◦◦———————

In mid-2005, after a twelve-year stint at that ad agency, I left to start my own business. The group I originally managed had a staff of three full-time employees, plus additional temporary workers when we needed to make our survey phone calls. Since market research at an ad agency is generally project-based, and not a full-time job, my group was losing money. We were paying people to sit around doing nothing productive. I fixed that by outsourcing most of the tasks. We only paid providers or individuals when we had projects going; just as we did for those temporary workers. The costs for the outsourced activities were factored into the project cost to the client, with a nice profit margin added in. By cutting that overheard, we went from being a major money drain to a highly profitable operation. I believed that adopting that model and striking out on my own made a great deal of sense. Although I continued to do some jobs for the agency, I called the shots as to how the work was done. It was scary, but after the initial anxiety wore off, tremendously satisfying.

To keep costs down, I set up shop in our home. After being employed by companies large and small for years, I was suddenly on my own. It caused some anxiety for David and me initially, he for financial reason, I for my ego. Once that passed, I grew to love the independence it afforded me. David was still working, so his money kept coming in. The worst we thought might happen was that I wouldn't get any clients and I'd retire early. I became an entrepreneur at fifty-nine.

Aside from the uncertainty of not getting a regular paycheck and working hard to get a solo consultancy business up and running, it was liberating. I quickly learned how to network effectively and built the business up from two initial clients to thirty-eight within the eight years I was in business. All of that practice prospecting at the agency was paying dividends. Fortunately, my thirty-eight clients didn't all have projects running at the same time. In fact, nine of them entrusted me with multiple projects over the years, so I was definitely doing something right.

I wasn't making a fortune, but that wasn't the major goal. I basically wanted to have much more flexibility in my life and complete management over how the work was done. Yes, my name is Mary Jo, and I'm a total control freak. In addition, I like to have things my way. David says I'm a spoiled brat, a frequent criticism of an only child. However, he liked having me home more, and was pleased at how much happier I was. I even made enough money that we didn't notice a significant impact on our lifestyle. Having my own research consultancy allowed me to manage my time far better than I could when I was working for others. Best of all, it eliminated my daily commute on Houston's infamous 610 Loop. I walked to work. Our dog, Riley, kept me company. I finally had the great boss I'd always wanted.

Since I could manage my time the way I wanted to, David and I got more serious about our Ancestry family tree. We tackled his family first, since we knew far more about them than we did about mine. He had two branches, mother, and father. I had one. That was when we discovered that genealogy, like home remodeling, is a disease. Once you start, you can never stop.

Never.

We're still working on it, many years later.

We also included our daughter-in-law's family in our growing tree. There were some interesting discoveries in Trish's family that she knew nothing about. I found that her distant ancestors were some of the earliest settlers of Virginia, and that they'd migrated down along the east coast and through North Carolina to eventually settle in Texas. Unlike my family, who lived in and around Philadelphia for centuries, or David's, who clustered in eastern, and later, western Pennsylvania, they were some of the adventurous souls and early explorers who battled the wild animals and wilder lands to settle this country.

Our small immediate family, David and I, our son, Mike, his wife, Trish, and their two children, Dale and Elise, is fortunate in not needing or wanting many material things. Finding good gifts for one another sometimes becomes a brain-wracking experience. One Christmas, while searching for a good gift for Trish, I came up with the idea of doing a family book. In addition to producing her family tree, David and I had found a lot of information on many of her ancestors, so it was mainly a matter of producing Microsoft Word documents and assembling all of the information we had. Thanks to Ancestry, some Googling, and the fact that her ancestors were people of some repute, I was able to fill a large three-ring binder with fairly detailed histories of some of them, particularly those who'd started out in Virginia and migrated to the Carolinas. I even developed a template with a leafless tree grayed out in the background, over which I could "type" information. Each page had a summary of who the person was, and which side of her family they were on—mother's or father's. Although it was certainly not the easiest gift to procure that I'd ever given to someone, it was surely the best.

Trish's mother was still living at the time, and she didn't know much of their family history either, so it turned out to be a double gift for two of our favorite women, plus a legacy for our two grandchildren, who will grow to appreciate family histories someday.

Like many of us with Colonial ancestry, Trish had several Revolutionary War Patriots in her family. Unlike most, one of them was a woman, Laodicea Langston, called Dicey by her family. Dicey, at the tender age of thirteen, performed valuable services to the American cause by spying on the British troops near their home in South Carolina. She pulled it off because none of the British suspected that a little girl would be spying on them. Shows what they knew. I even found a book about her, written by a distant cousin of Trish's. That family book and the story of Dicey was probably the best gift I've ever presented to anyone. While it left two strong women in tears, they were much better informed about their family. Even the kids thought it was pretty cool.

We found some fascinating history about David's family, including how they had to move around to avoid religious persecution. Europe in the 1600s was a hotbed of religious intolerance. According to the website of Dr. Gayle Olson-Raymer, who retired from teaching at Humboldt State University, "Every European nation during this time had an established church that mandated what form of religious worship and belief were acceptable. Most people believed that public order was dependent on everyone believing the same thing about religion and practiceing the same religious lifestyles. There was literally no thought of religion being a matter of private choice. Anyone who challenged the mandated form of religious worship faced persecution by both church authorities and the government that supported the church."

Although the Spanish Inquisition in the late 1400s gets a lot of bad press for religious intolerance, Germany and Switzerland were far worse. Between 1550 and 1650 in Germany, over 30,000 persecutions of alleged witches occurred. In 16th century Switzerland, people in one small remote area killed 3,300 of their fellow inhabitants for allegedly committing satanic crimes. In Wiesensteig, Germany, sixty-three women—alleged witches—were burned to death in one year[1]. Who were these witches? They were primarily women who did not adhere to the social, political, spiritual, and/or economic status quo. This went far beyond mere intolerance. You could lose your life if you thought differently than other people.

Naturally, there were massive population shifts back and forth between Germany and Switzerland, depending on which way the religious intolerance winds were

---

[1] Norman Cohn, *Europe's Inner Demons: An Inquiry Inspired by the Great Witch Hunt.* NY: Basic Books, 1975:254

blowing. All of this occurred after Martin Luther's Reformation in the early 1500s, when a host of Protestant religions was formed in opposition to the Catholic Church. David's family adhered to one of these, the Anabaptists. They were the forerunners of today's Mennonites.

His sixth great grandfather, Christian Martin, like many others, was jailed in Switzerland for his religious beliefs. Luckily, he was not killed, or David might not be here. Christian emigrated to America with one of his sons. He was sixty-three years old when he made that difficult journey across the Atlantic on the *Pink Plaisance*. These immigrants were the Palatines, so called because they came from the Palatinate or Middle Rhine region of southwestern Germany. Like many other Germans, they settled in Lancaster County in eastern Pennsylvania in what is now called Pennsylvania Dutch country. Christian lived there with his family for sixteen more years. There are still a lot of Martins in that part of Pennsylvania.

The Dutch is actually a misnomer. They were not Dutch, but German. The word Dutch comes from the German word Deutsch, meaning German. That caused some confusion for me for years, since my grandmother had told me when I was a child that her family was Dutch and Pennsylvania Dutch. That translates to German and German immigrants to Eastern Pennsylvania, as I now know. When we began our genealogy quest, I assumed her family had come from Holland, and wondered why I could never find any ancestors there.

Meanwhile, I half-heartedly worked on the one side I had, my mother's family, and got back more generations than I thought I would. Initially there was nothing startling or exciting. No one I found out about was ever jailed, which is probably a good thing. As is usual in genealogy, I hit dead ends I couldn't get past, became frustrated, and eventually stopped working so hard at it.

Fortunately, or unfortunately, I had paying work that kept me plenty busy. David, meanwhile, was forging ahead. He was finding those extraordinary things about religious persecution, and how his forebears made it out just in time. I have to admit it. I was jealous. He knew that. And he knew that I really wanted to understand something, anything, about my father and his family, so he searched for that as well as for people in his family.

Then one day, he yelled, "I found your father's social security number!"

At that moment, I was overloaded with a big project. I replied, "Wow! That's interesting. Maybe it will allow us to get more information about him. As soon as I get this project under control, we'll have to dig some more."

That social security number didn't really tell us anything at the time, but it would lead us to an information bonanza later.

Although we went to a genealogy library a few times, most of our work was done on the internet. How we ever lived without it is a mystery. In genealogy, it gives us access to things that would have taken years and multiple library, courthouse, church, and cemetery trips to find.

As a market researcher, searching the internet was second nature for me. In addition, it was fun to be a family detective, satisfy my urge for nearly instantaneous results, and discover exciting things about our ancestors.

Sometimes, though, you just have to turn to "hard copy" resources. Houston genealogists are fortunate to have The Clayton Library in the city's Museum District. This is the place to go when online sources are mute on a person or a family branch. In addition to a large collection of books, they have microfilm and microfiche records and can access information from the Mormon Church's vast genealogical library in Salt Lake City. It is one of the top genealogy libraries in the country, and we're lucky enough to have it here.

We did find some things at The Clayton, especially on David's family, on whom several books have been written. My family, not so much. Apparently, no one took the time or had any interest in writing about my ancestors. After finding some of the things I have, I have to wonder why, since I now know that there are some fascinating stories there. Apparently, that will be up to me.

Chapter Four

Early Days

"Your memories from your early childhood seem to have such purchase on your emotions. They are so concrete."
DANA SPIOTTA

I grew up in a single-parent household. My mother, Irene, and I lived with my grandparents in a small row house on a quiet street in South Philadelphia. It was the epitome of urban. Lots of cement, very little grass. We had one tree on our block, a big, beautiful sycamore that produced little spiky balls each fall. They were great for throwing at each other in mock battles. That was my idea of nature.

There was an elementary school and a junior high across the street from us where I went to classes from kindergarten through grade nine. The property included a large school yard, excellent for summer programs, where I learned how to walk on stilts and make crafty things like ashtrays and potholders. There were also smooth surfaces for riding a bike or a scooter and drawing out hopscotch games with chalk.

What kind of amusements did an inner-city kid have on a long, sultry summer day before electronics? Actually, a lot. There was a game called steps (sometimes termed heaven, where you had to answer questions correctly to move up the steps), hopscotch, jacks, and pick-up sticks. Or you could catch a cool breeze by skating or riding your bike fast. If the heat got too oppressive, someone would invariably open a fire plug and push their rump up against the water coming out to create a shower. That was great until a neighbor would rat us out and a fireman would come turn it off. Then there was Deadbox. The goal was to get your cap from box one through box twelve, without getting it in the central "Deadbox." Those games could take hours and there were always contests between the boys—who thought they were the experts—and the girls, who had better aim. For those of you unlucky enough to not have grown up in South Philadelphia, here's how we played it:

1. Starting with our favorite bottle cap (soda—or beer if your parents drank it), the first player placed his cap in box 1. Everyone had their favorite, or lucky cap.

2. We got down on one knee and flicked our middle finger against our thumb to propel the cap from box 1 to box 2. And so on. The cap had to land completely in the box, not on a line. If not, you started again.

3. If your cap landed in the Deadbox, or an opponent knocked your cap out of a box, you had to start again.

4. The first player to get through all the boxes was the winner.

My mother dragged me to every museum in the city, so I knew them all. We did the well-known, popular ones like the Art Museum, The Franklin Institute, The Academy of Natural Sciences, and, of course, all the historic sites. As you might imagine, there are a lot of those in Philadelphia.

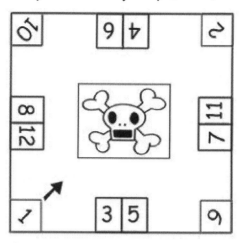

A drawing of a Deadbox field. More complex games had two additional boxes—thirteen and fourteen—which were on the short edges of the deadbox. Those were smaller and were killers. Permission to reproduce from the South Philly Memoirs Blog.

One of my favorites in that category was Betsy Ross's house, which was on a street called Elfreth's Alley. The street and the house were small, as were most things from that time. We never had a car, so to get anywhere, we took buses, trolleys, trackless trolleys, or subways. I vividly recall going to a small museum called The Atwater Kent Museum; I think that except for my mother and me, no one had ever heard of it. Now called the Philadelphia History Museum, I remember it having a lot of dioramas and small models of things, including some that were mechanical or electrified and moved or lit up when you pushed a button or two. It doesn't seem to have any exhibits like that now, based on their website. But then, I don't resemble anything I looked like then either.

As I got older and able to take trolleys and buses by myself (kids could do that back then), I went on summer field trips with the Academy of Natural Sciences, one of my favorite places. The Academy of Natural Sciences taught me that nature was more than the patch of bachelor buttons and nasturtiums I planted in our small back yard, and the box turtle who wandered in one year and decided to stay with us.

Philadelphia has some excellent parks and wild spaces. Wissahickon Creek, a tributary of the Schuylkill River and part of the huge Fairmont Park system, was my favorite. The name comes from the Lenape Indian word wiessahitkonk, for "catfish creek" or "stream of yellowish color." A group of us pre-teens would go tromping through the woods, sweating in the hot, humid Philadelphia summers, led by a naturalist who taught us the differences between frogs and toads, moths and butterflies, and revealed the mysteries of catching salamanders and crayfish. Only after we moved to Texas did I find out that crayfish are the same thing as crawfish and you can eat them. All those years I missed eating those delectable little crustaceans.

Those field trips also afforded us girls the chance to be close to cute boys. There was one I was especially smitten with, named Hugh. He looked like a typical British boy—although he was American—and I used salamander and crawfish hunting as an excuse to get near him. The only problem was his sister, whose name I can't remember since she wasn't important to me at all. In fact, she tended to get in the way many times, thwarting my efforts. Sadly, Hugh wasn't the least bit interested in me, or any other girl, for that matter. He was a serious junior naturalist. He likely ended up as a biologist when he grew up.

David later taught me what nature was really like when we began camping. It was an eye-opener to discover that tents leak in the rain if you touch the fabric with your finger—or your foot. Cooking at a campsite is not what it's cracked up to be either. Movies and ads always make it look so romantic. Until you find yourself trying to make breakfast in July while it's snowing, as it did on one trip to the Canadian Rockies. As I've told you, I'm a city kid, born and raised on concrete, and although I loved being out in nature, I didn't like living in it. Having to battle all kinds of bugs, and possibly snakes, experiencing the joy of hikes to a restroom in the middle of the night, where you might encounter a skunk, smelling like smoke from campfires, and never feeling totally clean, were not my idea of fun. Still, it allowed us to have inexpensive vacations in some beautiful locations and see a lot of this country and Canada.

In my genealogy work, I've learned that the neighborhood where I grew up was very close to the areas of South Philadelphia in which many people in my mother's family had lived for generations. Unlike Trish's family, who migrated over large distances along the east coast and into Texas, mine were homebodies.

My grandmother Irene, like my mother, Irene, who was named for her, and who I called Nana, was the matriarch of the family. She had crippling rheumatoid arthritis, was bedridden, and cared for by my mother. Since Nana wasn't mobile, our home was the epicenter for visits from my mother's two brothers, Sam and Frank, and their wives and children, plus occasional visits of multitudes of second and third cousins. When they visited, I heard stories of distant relatives, and only wish now that I'd documented them then. Generally, kids don't appreciate the value of those stories. It's only as we get older that they begin to have meaning. As I do genealogy, I sometimes have flashbacks when I find something about someone that I'd known but had totally forgotten about. I try to document those things for our grandchildren. Hopefully, someday they'll find them interesting and appreciate my efforts.

Nana, aka Irene Wilson Benckert Phillippe
(in the 1920s). Personal photo.

What I do recall hearing about were the Baker ancestors, who were related on my grandfather's side. They apparently had a higher social standing than we did, were written up in the "society pages" of the papers in Philadelphia and New York and had more money than my immediate family did. That probably wouldn't have been hard to do. We four lived on Social Security and a pension from the City of Philadelphia, where my grandfather had worked as a Deputy Real Estate Assessor.

Chapter Five

Another Effect of Familial Tremor

*"Music is a moral law. It gives soul to the universe,
wings to the mind, flight to the imagination,
and charm and gaiety to life and to everything."*
PLATO

As a child, I loved to sing. It took a while for me to notice that this was also affected by familial tremor. I could no longer sing; at least not well. This upset me immensely. When I was younger, I sang in our church choir and in South Philadelphia High School's (SPHS) A Cappella Choir. In our SPHS choir, we performed a range of pieces, from works by Bach, Mozart, Vivaldi, and Handel, to classic gospel pieces like *"Oh, What a Beautiful City,"* and an occasional sprinkling of more modern composers. We performed all over the city of Philadelphia, and I still fondly recall singing before live audiences at Philadelphia's City Hall and at what was then the Wanamaker department store during the holidays.

Apparently, I must have been pretty good, since I was invited to try out for the All-City Choir, composed of singers from schools across the entire Philadelphia metropolitan area. I had to audition, and it was a great honor to be selected. We even performed on the stage of The Academy of Music (now part of the Kimmel Center for the Performing Arts), an awesome experience. In addition, I, a humble first alto, was one of the soloists in *Amahl and the Night Visitors*. They recorded the performance—on vinyl, of course—and I recently had that converted to a CD so it might have a better chance of surviving a longer time.

My mother and I attended services at Gloria Dei (Old Swedes') Church, one of the oldest places of worship in the country, where I was in the choir. My family had a long history with the church, with many of my ancestors christened, married, and eventually buried, at the church. Like many places in the Northeastern part of the country, history oozed from every brick and cobblestone in Philadelphia. I suspect the major reason I went to church was that I loved the music so much. It was important for my mother, too. In Philadelphia, good families were Episcopalians, and had an established history. We fit into that category easily and it validated her legitimacy—and mine.

Swedish colonists established Gloria Dei in 1677, five years before the founding of Philadelphia. The church has maintained many Swedish traditions. One of them is the Lucia Fest, a custom that is a mixture of Christianity and paganism. It celebrates both the birth of the Christ child and the winter solstice.

Because Lucia lived before written historical documents existed, her story is based on oral histories. While there are multiple versions, this one most closely follows the Swedish version. Sankta Lucia, or St. Lucy, was born in Syracuse, Sicily around 283AD and died in 303AD. The tale is told that her parents preferred that she marry a man whom she didn't want to wed. After seeing an angel, while praying at a shrine for her sick mother, she converted to Christianity. She decided to remain a virgin and devote her life to helping the poor rather than marry an old man she knew nothing of. She was burned at the stake for her efforts.

The winter solstice connection to the Lucia fest is based on the timing in the old Julian calendar, when the shortest, darkest day of the year was December thirteenth, rather than our current date of December twenty-first.

The Lucia fest at Gloria Dei was, and still is, a beautiful enactment. From the entirely candle-lit church, it begins with a procession of little boys and girls dressed in red as *tomptegubbars* (Santa's elves), followed by the *stjärngossar* (star boys), and Lucia's court of young girls dressed in long white nightgowns with green wreaths on their heads, carrying lighted candles. Finally, they are followed by the girl chosen to be Lucia. All of the participants sing traditional Swedish songs a capella as they proceed down the aisle of the church. Just thinking and writing about it gives me goosebumps. At the old building that was Gloria Dei, besides the performers and the audience, there were a lot of unobtrusive firefighters on the scene, just in case.

In homes throughout Sweden—and parts of the US where there are many Swedish immigrants—the custom is for the oldest girl in the household to arise early and walk through her house on the day of the solstice. She wakes her family, serving sweetbreads and coffee, singing along the way. Lucia represents the lengthening of the days and the return of the sun. And, later, the arrival of the Christ child, as the light of the world. In my sixteenth year, I was chosen to be a Lucia. I sang solo in Swedish while wearing a crown of seven lighted candles, signifying the seven known planets at the time this custom began. Even after all these years, I still remember the words. In spite of being scary, it was also exhilarating.

The author as Lucia with my mom, dressed in traditional Swedish folk costume. Those candles were wax, they were lit, and there were no saucers to catch the dripping wax, so my court and I spent time picking congealed wax out of my hair and off my nightgown after the performance. Personal photo.

Singing filled a significant part of my early life, and I could no longer do it. Not even singing happy birthday. It was a major loss for me. The speech therapy I did helped my speaking voice. But I was still so distraught about my inability to sing at all that the neurologist who first diagnosed the familial tremor suggested I see an ear, nose, and throat specialist who focused solely on vocal problems. Singers from all over the country come to him for help; many of them are prominent cast members from the Houston Grand Opera. Dr. Stasney performed a battery of tests on me and did still and video photography to determine the cause of my vocal tremor. Fortunately, he did not find any physical abnormalities. While the speech therapy helped the shake in my speaking voice somewhat, it did nothing for my singing. I feared that chapter of my life was over for good.

Chapter Six

Aunt Mary & Josephine and the DAR (Daughters of the American Revolution) Connection

"When we illuminate the road back to our ancestors, they have a way of reaching out, of manifesting themselves...sometimes even physically."
RAQUEL CEPEDA

One of my grandfather's cousins (first, one time re-moved), was Daniel Clifton Baker McLearn, or as I knew him, Uncle Cliff. He was the son of one of those "Baker girls," Josephine Clifton Baker. She was a sister of Margaret Cushing Baker, my grandfather's grandmother. I know, this gets confusing. I've included a small section of my family tree at the end of this book, in case you really want to understand these connections.

Uncle Cliff was my Godfather, and his wife and their daughter were my Godmothers. He visited fairly often along with his wife, Mary Alley, who was from Atlanta, and their daughter, Josephine. I always loved to see Uncle Cliff. He brought along with him a cheery disposition and had a constant twinkle in his eye. I was sure he was always up to something.

The author as a girl with Uncle Cliff (left) and my grandfather (right). Apparently, I was explaining something interesting or complex to Uncle Cliff. Although not Italian, I have always talked with my hands. Maybe it was the neighborhood where we lived, composed mostly of families of Italian descent. I recall Uncle Cliff giving me that little outfit. I loved it. Personal photo.

Aunt Mary had a keen interest in genealogy, along with a strong Georgia accent, which my mother and grand-mother mimicked and snickered about after their visits. I never understood how they could be so mean. It was totally out of character for these two loving, caring women. It was only years later that I began to see that they had some serious judgmental sides. Aunt Mary and her daughter were always very kind to me and were intrepid genealogists. I enjoyed their visits immensely and loved hearing them tell family stories.

They both did a lot of research (the hard way back then) and found that we had a Revolutionary War Patriot in our family. Having a Patriot in your lineage means that you are eligible to join the DAR (Daughters of the American Revolution). I now know quite a lot about those Baker girls and learned that all of them had been DAR members, including Uncle Cliff's mother. His daughter, Josephine, joined the DAR based on her father's ancestry. Of course, Aunt Mary and Josephine were convinced that I had to apply too. I was a kid back then. What did I care about the DAR? Of course, I never did anything about it. At least not then.

In spite of my teenage attitude, I always remembered some of the stories they told—like the Revolutionary War Patriot, the Mayflower connection, and the ancestors who were buried in the graveyard of Gloria Dei Church. One of those graves was a raised tomb, and we used to sit on it before services. The family joked about it; we were sitting on our ancestors. I now have documentation on the occupants of the tomb, proving that is indeed the case.

I've subsequently been able to authenticate those family stories surrounding my church, including records of family members who attended services or were married or buried there. Aunt Mary and Josephine knew what they were talking about. In spite of that, in all of my years of searching, I've never found that Mayflower connection, except by one of the Baker girl's marriage. I'm not sure what you think, but in my mind, that doesn't count. Then again, maybe there's something I just haven't found yet. This is what makes genealogy so much fun. There's always a little nugget out there just waiting to be unearthed.

*Mary (right) and Josephine (left) McLearn
with the author (center). Personal photo.*

I've subsequently learned a lot about my Revolutionary War patriot. He was a Private in the Delaware Militia, 1st Battalion, New Castle County, and served in the Battle of Camden, in South Carolina, where he was severely wounded. David and I were driving back home to Houston from the Outer Banks of North Carolina several years ago, when we happened to see a sign near Camden, South Carolina for a Revolutionary War battlefield. Since we weren't in a hurry, we decided to stop. That battlefield turned out to be the one in which my 5th great grandfather, John Clifton, fought against the British. I was actually in the spot where one of my ancestors fought for American freedom and was wounded. Thankfully for me, unlike many of his fellow soldiers, he was not killed. Sadly, the Battle of Camden was one of the few encounters during the Revolutionary War in which the Americans were soundly defeated. It gives me the chills when I think about it.

I remember Aunt Mary and Josephine fondly, and wish they were still with us, or that I'd listened more attentively as a child. But their spirits live on in me as a serious genealogist. I think they'd be proud of my efforts and my ultimately joining the DAR. I did that primarily to help me unlock some roadblocks I'd encountered. I was able to easily prove my lineage, because those Baker girls and others in my family were members nearly a century before I applied.

In the process of gathering documentation for my Revolutionary War connection closer in time, I made one horrific discovery that no one in my family ever talked about. Working with a local DAR member to document my more recent lineage, we found a death certificate for my great-grandfather, Samuel Phillippe, my mother's father's father. It listed his cause of death as "pistol shot wounds self-inflicted while temporarily insane." It gave me the hollow feeling you get in the pit of your stomach when you learn something terrible. I still get that feeling if I think about it. I wish I understood what drove him to commit suicide, but I realize I never will. There's no one left who might know or would tell.

Chapter Seven

Aunt Carrie—and Things That Nice Girls Didn't Do Back Then

"...but never try to answer for what is between a husband and his wife, or a lover and his mistress. There is always one little corner which remains hidden from all the world and is known only to the two of them."
FYODOR DOSTOYEVSKY

My searching also unearthed a scandalous family tale that I knew only parts of when I was growing up. Apparently, I got the rigorously edited version. My mother often spoke lovingly about her Great Aunt Carrie. Aunt Carrie was the daughter of one of those Baker girls, and she and my mother were very close. I'm lucky enough to have some of her beautiful jewelry, which she passed on to my mom, and my mom passed on to me. I wear it as often as I can and I cherish and enjoy it immensely.

I found in my genealogy wanderings that Aunt Carrie had been married and had a child named Marion. Marion died in 1909, when she was only twelve years old. I've only recently found the cause of her death—spinal meningitis, secondary to otitis media, a common ear infection. Our son had repeated bouts of ear infections when he was young. Unlike Mike's experience, Marion's illness occurred years before the use of antibiotics, which could have quickly and easily saved her life.

Marion Price. Permission to reproduce from The Rosenbach Museum and Library.

I suspect my mother, who was born in 1912, became something of a surrogate daughter for Aunt Carrie. After Marion's death, it seems that Aunt Carrie's marriage fell apart. Although there is no divorce record, her husband apparently left Philadelphia and the census record from 1930 shows him living in Detroit, and his marital status as a widower. Strange until you remember that census data is self-reported. His death certificate appears in 1932 in Detroit. His obituary doesn't say what he did for a living, simply that he was "employed in various automobile factories." That 1930 census record shows him as a roomer in someone else's home and lists his occupation as a stock manager. This seems to be quite a comedown for a Princeton man who lettered in baseball and football, had Mayflower ancestry, and went on to become Assistant City Editor at the Philadelphia Times newspaper.

A young Carrie Price. Personal photo.

That isn't the most interesting thing I learned about Aunt Carrie. In doing genealogy, it's good to use sources other than Ancestry or other genealogical sites. One day, I did a search on everyone's favorite search engine, Google, for Aunt Carrie's name, and found a book review in an issue of Time magazine from the early 1960s. The review was for a biography of a man named Dr. Abraham Simon Wolf Rosenbach. In this review, she was mentioned as the mistress of forty years of the man who was often referred to as "Doc" Rosenbach. Wow! That certainly threw me for a loop. I'd heard my mother talk about Doc Rosenbach, but no one had ever told me about Aunt Carrie being his mistress. That was only one of the things I'd never been told.

The Doc appellation came from Rosenbach's PhD in English Literature from the University of Pennsylvania. Instead of pursuing an academic life, where he would have been paid inadequately, he became a famous dealer in rare books and manuscripts, including Shakespearean folios and first editions. He lived in Philadelphia and had shops there and in New York. The shop in Philadelphia was in a very fashionable neighborhood on Delancey Street, near

Rittenhouse Square, and the New York shop was on Madison Avenue. Both were socially acceptable addresses, where the types of wealthy clients he dealt with were quite comfortable.

Doc's home and the shop in Philadelphia is now the Rosenbach Museum and Library, part of the Free Library of Philadelphia, where some of the works he acquired are on display. A couple of years ago, I was on a trip to Philadelphia for my 50th high school reunion and was fortunate enough to visit the museum and taken on a private tour. It was a wonderful experience; I was treated like royalty. I saw first editions of Shakespeare folios, a first edition of James Joyce's *Ulysses*, first editions of Marianne Moore's poems, and a huge collection of other invaluable rare books.

The best part was seeing some documents and photographs of Aunt Carrie, and, most impressive of all, a large oil portrait of her when she was older than she was in the family photographs I had. Doc's brother, Philip, dealt in

Carrie Price Portrait. Permission to reproduce from The Rosenbach Museum and Library.

antique furniture and accessories, and at one time, this portrait had a prominent place in Philip's shop.

To give you a better idea of the people Doc had as clients, one was Harry Widener, an American business-man and bibliophile, and a member of the prominent Philadelphia Widener family. Harry was a passenger on the HMS Titanic, along with his mother and father, his mother's maid, and his father's valet. His mother and her maid were rescued, but Harry, his father, and his father's valet perished. After their deaths, his mother donated $2 million to establish Harvard University's Widener Memorial Library in his memory. Widener's collection of books—many acquired by Doc Rosenbach—formed the nucleus of Harvard's Widener Library.

Doc and Aunt Carrie were quite an item; one that "nice" people didn't talk about back then. His family was strict Orthodox Jewish, and Aunt Carrie was an Episcopalian, so they could never marry—his family would not have stood for that. Apparently, Doc and Aunt Carrie were deeply in love, so they did the next best thing. They lived surrepti-tiously as lovers, he in his home, she in hers.

Doc had a summer house in Strathmere, New Jersey, on the southern Jersey shore. As did Aunt Carrie. It's where they escaped the hot, humid Philadelphia weather, and possibly the judgmental people they encountered there. They fished often and had fish fries with their catches. My mother was invited to both Doc's home in Philadelphia and to "The Boathouse," as his home in Strathmere was called.

I learned much more about Aunt Carrie than the highly-edited version I'd heard as a child and found it fascinating. She stayed busy serving her summer com-munity by organizing the Red Cross in Strathmere. In

*The Interior of The Boathouse. Permission to reproduce from
The Rosenbach Museum and Library.*

The Boathouse, she provided an emergency hospital at her own expense to take care of shipwrecked sailors, organized the lifeguards, was active in the American Shore and Beach Preservation Association and was a life member of the Cape May Historical Society. In addition, she was chief air raid warden of the Strathmere region. No one ever told me any of these wonderful stories about her. She died just two years before I was born. I only wish I'd had a chance to know her.

My Mom, Irene, with two big flounders,
in front of The Boathouse. Personal photo.

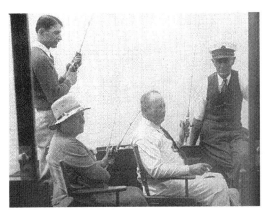

Aunt Carrie, Doc Rosenbach, Captain Maxwell, and
an unidentified friend, fishing in New Jersey on Doc's boat,
The First Folio. Permission to reproduce from
The Rosenbach Museum and Library.

Part Two

Discoveries

"Some beautiful paths can't be
discovered without getting lost."
Erol Ozan

Chapter Eight

The First Discovery

"I am a cage, in search of a bird."
Franz Kafka

Back to the search for my father's history and roots. That social security number David found for him reignited my desire to find out more about him and his family. Of course, I wanted to be able to solve my medical mystery and having another bit of data got my hopes up. Once I wrapped up the paying project that was keeping me busy, I became infected with the genealogy disease again.

Having my father's social security number helped us discover that we had his middle name wrong. It was also wrong on my birth certificate. That was a clue that suggested something to us about the circumstances of my birth. I suspect that my mother may never have told my father about me. In addition, he most likely was not present when the hospital collected information about the parents, or he probably would have corrected his middle name. The fact that it was wrong on the birth certificate could mean either that my mother didn't know his correct middle name, or maybe she just got it wrong. Although I'll never know this with any certainty, I don't believe he was ever aware of my existence.

As good as it was to find it, that social security number didn't tell me anything about my father's medical history. Nor did it give me any insights into what kind of a person he was—where and how he grew up, how he got into the Navy, and how he and my mother met.

I had one small clue, but it wasn't that useful. It would, however, lead to a much more useful source and some big surprises later.

Chapter Nine

Thanks for Navy Records

*"It is a capital mistake to theorize before one has data.
Insensibly one begins to twist facts to suit theories, instead of
theories to suit facts."*
Arthur Conan Doyle

Armed with my father's social security number, I began my search. Initially, I uncovered some information about his long-ago family on Ancestry. This genealogical treasure trove led me to US Census and other data sources, and to other people's family trees. Fortunately, some of them were well-documented, so I could trust what was contained in them. It allowed me to go back in time on his father's side and gave me a smattering of some intriguing genealogical information.

Hundreds of years ago, ancestors on my father's side had come from Yorkshire, England, in an area called Bolton-by-Bowland, where they had lived for centuries. David always told me he suspected I was a Limey, and this proved it. Plus, I like gin. His guess was probably not surprising with a name like Latham. Although, as with many others, the spelling changed over the years, from Laythum to Laytham, and eventually to Latham. That surname is very common in Yorkshire, even to this day. I had this confirmed in a tourist office in Barcelona, Spain while we were on a vacation, when I struck up a conversation with a woman who happened to be from Yorkshire. No, we're not cousins; we checked that out. Once again, it showed that it truly is a small world.

While I had some luck on his father's side, his mother's family was initially a dead end. Her maiden name was Jones, so rather than finding too little information, I found too many possibilities. It wasn't until much later that I was able to break through that brick wall, after I discovered I had her birthplace wrong. Once I had that right, I found that her family was German and Dutch, and emigrated to America centuries ago. Like our daughter-in-law, Trish's family, my ancestors on that side settled the wilderness in the Carolinas, Tennessee, and eventually found their way to Kentucky. That's where she met my grandfather, Thomas Latham. One of my ancestors, John Shell, set up and operated the first water mill on Greasy Creek in Leslie County, Kentucky. He was a busy man, operating a small country store, and was a bee keeper, a blacksmith, a gunsmith, and a fanner (someone who separates the grain from the chaff). The legend is that he lived to be 134 years old. As you might imagine, there's some debate about that.

Unfortunately, as with many explorations in genealogy, although I'd unearthed the skeleton of my father's family, there was very little meat on those bones. Just basic facts, like birth and death dates and marriage, christening, and burial data. And, naturally, there was no information on medical problems. While it got me closer to my ancestry than that 180,000-year-old African adventurer, it provided no insights into my father's background other than where he'd lived, from US Census data. Most importantly, his medical history remained a blank page.

After searching for other sources, I realized that the Navy must have personnel records. With some non-Ancestry web crawling, I learned how I could get that detailed information. I also discovered that the branches of the US armed services maintain records for a very long time. Some of them are the sources of the military data that's on Ancestry, and many of them go back to the Revolutionary War. For me, that was a terrific finding. Although some of the documents are on the web now and a number are available on Ancestry, I was seeking out much more detailed information which only family members could access.

Fortunately, my father's name was on my birth certificate, even if his middle name was apparently incorrect. It showed there as Edward, while his Social Security record indicated that it is really Everett. The Everett middle name came from the last name of Thomas' boss and owner of the machine shop where he worked—Isaac Everett. Isaac's ancestors had been some of the early founders of Louisville and had a history of philanthropy. Unlike Isaac, Clarence's parents were poor, and Clarence was the baby—the last of their ten children. When Thomas' children were born, Isaac gave Thomas a bonus, based on his good work history, and because Isaac was a good man who didn't want to see other good men struggle.

From the BuPers (the Bureau of Personnel) website of the US Navy, I learned how I could get my father's complete service records. All I needed to do was fill out and send them a form, along with a registered copy of my birth certificate, and the Navy would send me a copy of his service records. Excitedly, I filled out the form. I found a wonderful web source, VitalCheck, which for a reasonable fee, will get you a registered copy of your birth certificate, and sent everything off to the Naval records department in St. Louis. At the time, I didn't know that separate archives were kept for medical records. I found that out later.

Then I waited. And waited. By this time, I was convinced I was hot on the trail, certain I'd get all the answers I was looking for. Although I'm getting somewhat better as I get older, I've never been a very patient person. My "patience fuse" in this case was even shorter than usual. As with all things bureaucratic, you cannot hurry the process.

Finally, after about three to four weeks, I got a huge package in the mail. It was roughly two inches thick. I started at the top and worked my way down the pile. Sifting through that river of paper was like panning for gold nuggets. It contained records of my father's immediate family, including names and addresses for his parents, Thomas and Dora. I learned that he'd worked in a drug store in Louisville, Kentucky in civilian life, and had been born on the fourth of July. He was not tall, measuring five feet six inches when he enlisted, and was neither underweight nor overweight. He had dark brown curly hair and blue eyes. Apparently, my guess at his eye color from that old grainy black and white photo was correct. My father attended Pharmacy and Dental technician schools in addition to the usual military training in the Navy. He got middle-of-the road grades, but passed everything except rifle instruction, which he had to repeat. Funny, you'd think a boy from Kentucky could shoot.

Reading through those records was like a trip back in time to a period in our country's history that few people alive today can relate to. I certainly couldn't. My generation had heard stories about what it was like to go through World War II from our parents, and many of us were touched to some extent by the Korean War. Of course, Vietnam was a pivotal point for many of us Baby Boomers during our impressionable, idealistic years, and we protested while losing many fine, young men in that "conflict." Vietnam was not anything like WWII, which was the largest armed conflict in history, and produced people referred to by the now-retired NBC broadcaster, Tom Brokaw, as "The Greatest Generation". Their values and beliefs were very different than those of us Baby Boomers. My dad was one of them. And so was my mom.

The biggest disappointment in those Naval records was that there was nothing about his medical history. I still knew nothing about my familial tremor. But, I learned a lot of his background, including some things in his disciplinary records I'd rather not have found out about. Beyond the usual AOL (absent over leave) infractions, he was once accused of stealing from a fellow shipmate. Further down the pile, I was relieved to learn that he was later exonerated. He was also found D&D (drunk and disorderly) once in women's clothes. A side effect, no doubt, of a wild drunken binge with his buddies and some floozies they'd encountered. I began to get a feel for my father as a person during a difficult time in our country's history and the early part of his adult life. He was certainly no saint. My daddy was a bad boy. It was fascinating.

Most importantly, his files contained beneficiary designations. Initially, the beneficiaries were his parents, but as I got deeper into the stack, I found a wife and a child—

a girl, a half-sister! For the first time in my life, I was not a loner. I was no longer an only child. It took me sixty-two years to find this out. The feelings that this discovery aroused in me are nearly indescribable. They ranged from shock to excitement, to one of the greatest feelings of fulfillment I'd ever experienced.

I remember telling David, "You won't believe this! I have an older half-sister named Carolyn."

He just smiled and said, "I wonder if she knows more about your dad than you do?"

"That wouldn't be too hard to do," I grinned.

David responded, "Seriously, this could end your searching for your medical history."

"I certainly hope so," I said with fingers crossed.

Now I wondered what to do with this newfound information. Maybe this older sister might know something about our father's medical history...

Chapter Ten

Finding an Older Sister

"Being brave is when you have to do something because you know it is right, but at the same time, you are afraid to do it, because it might hurt or whatever. But you do it anyway."
MEG CABOT

I had a sister's name, a birth date, and no idea how to find her. Fortune shone down upon me in the form of a fellow genealogist, Alice, who turned out to be a distant cousin of my newfound sister on her mother's side. I have found many of those distant relatives doing genealogy. For instance, numerous cousins on my mother's side helped me fill in stories about those "Baker girls" that my mother never told me. I sent Alice an email, telling her what I needed. Unlike the Navy, the next day she had my brand-new sister's married name, an address, and, best of all, a telephone number. She was a true family detective and a top-notch genealogist.

Although this was great news for me, it illustrates how cautious you have to be online. There are databases that are readily accessible with information about all of us. For a small fee, you can even get criminal and civil records on people. The lesson is to be very careful what you put out there if you have any concerns about protecting your privacy.

Now I was in a quandary—how does one contact someone who possibly has no idea she has a half-sister? I thought about writing a letter, but I wanted a quick answer. Remember, I'm not a patient person. In addition, I had a telephone number. That would make a response much faster.

Then I thought about the fact that this sister is five years older than I am. What if she had a heart condition? How awful would it be to call someone to tell them you're their half-sister only to have them keel over from the shock of it? I wasn't sure I could live with that.

As a result, I sat and stewed on this for close to two months. Finally, I decided that I simply had to take the chance. If she hung up on me, or thought I was some kind of nut, so be it. I just had to try. And I had to take a risk and hope she was in good health.

Ultimately, on one hot, sunny June day, I sat in my comfortable, air-conditioned office, worked up my courage, and called the number. A man answered.

I asked, with my shaky voice even shakier from nervousness, "May I speak with Carolyn, please?"

He appeared to hesitate a lot longer than I thought he should, which told me that he was likely a bit suspicious. I'm sure mine was a voice he didn't recognize, but he finally said, "Yes, hold on please."

That was the easy part. Finally, I had her on the line. My heart was thumping as if it would jump out of my chest. Now I hoped I wouldn't keel over.

I am used to approaching and initiating conversations with anyone in a business or social situation. I'm actually quite good at it. By contrast, this was personal—completely uncharted territory.

Since I didn't know any other way to say it, I simply told her, "Hi, Carolyn! My name is Mary Jo Martin, and I believe that we are sisters."

There was a dead silence on the other end of the line. Fortunately, I didn't hear a thump, so I assumed she hadn't fallen over from the shock.

Then she said, "Oh." Nothing else, just "Oh." The tone was of someone who was just barely above speechless. In all fairness, I suppose I shouldn't have expected much else. How often do you get a phone call from a stranger who claims she's your sister? I'd likely do the same thing.

I couldn't just leave her with a bare fact, so explained, "Like you, my father was Clarence Everett Latham. He met my mother in 1945, and I am the result."

Again, she said, "Oh." Yet this time her tone indicated a bit more interest.

I then went on, explaining to what seemed like a dead telephone line, "I'm calling you because I have recently been diagnosed with a medical condition that I am told is hereditary. No one on my mother's side had this problem, so I assumed it had to come from my father's family. I'm looking for medical information on him and his people."

Once again, I got an "Oh" in response. By this time, I was beginning to feel that I was speaking to a broken, uncaring record. Or, to be fair, someone in shock.

At last, I think she'd gotten over her initial astonishment. She opened up and said, "Gosh, I don't think I can help you at all. He and my mother were divorced when I was about four years old, and I never really knew him or anyone in his family."

Thump. All those hopes dashed. It was like sitting down and hitting a chair that was lower than you expected it to be.

We talked some more (with me doing most of the talking), and she asked how I'd found her, so I had to tell her the whole story, from genealogy to Naval records. I said that I'd found a distant cousin of hers on her mother's side, and she was the one who found her telephone number for me. She appeared to be astonished that you could find that kind of information so easily. We had a nice (but I felt somewhat strained) conversation.

Finally, she said: "Wouldn't it be neat if we could meet sometime?" She followed that with a revelation, "Wow! I guess this means I'm not an only child anymore!"

I think she was recovering from the initial shock.

"Me too. It only took me sixty-two years to find this out."

Her eventual response and desire to get together made me feel really warm inside. I had a sister, and she wanted to meet me. It was an astonishing epiphany for a little, insecure person who'd grown up as an only child. I suspected it might mean the same thing to Carolyn.

I agreed it would be great if we could meet. Distance is a challenge for us. I'm in Texas, and she's in Washington state. While I love to travel, Carolyn is much more of a homebody, so I suppose it will be up to me to go see her. For a variety of reasons, neither of us has made that trip yet. But, we keep in touch pretty regularly.

I promised to send her whatever information I had, and she did the same. I mailed her a big envelope with a copy of our father's Naval records, and she sent me some photographs of him with her and her mom when she was a little girl. That was pretty much all she knew of him. Like my mother, Carolyn's mom would never speak about our father either.

We talked a while about our husbands and children, shared some grandchildren stories, and decided we should stay in touch.

Although I had discovered family, I was still no closer to knowing anything about my father or his medical history. Then I went back to that Navy records website and found out that there are separate records for medical history. I guess I should have looked more carefully the first time. That's the downside of limited patience. Sometimes you jump too fast. Once again, I filled out a form, sent it off to the Navy, and waited. And waited. Just like the last time. Some three to four weeks later, I got an even bigger package with my father's medical history.

I learned that he had passed away in 1991, so there was no chance I'd ever meet him. Frankly, I had mixed emotions about not being able to actually get to know him. The curious side of me wanted to actually see this man who had charmed my mother and contributed to my existence. I wondered if I looked at all like him. When I was a kid, people always told me I looked like my mother. I could never see it. So, whom did I look like? My analytical, reasoning side warned me that excavating old ghosts does not always turn out well. In addition, I had no idea how he'd react. He might reject me, which would have been devastating. Not only would I have felt like that weird kid who grew up without a father, but he might also tell me he didn't believe me and wanted no part of me. I didn't think I could handle that.

Perhaps the most disturbing part of those records was reading about his health issues and how he died. He was a lifelong smoker, and although he didn't have lung cancer, he did have cancer of the esophagus, which may be worse, since part of the treatment involved removing his larynx.

While cancer treatment then was not what it is today, esophageal cancer is one that is still particularly deadly. He battled a horrible disease, and he couldn't even talk about it. In addition, his wife at the time was not with him often. He was in the Madigan Army Hospital near Tacoma, Washington, nearly 100 miles from where they lived, on Whidbey Island, off the coast of Seattle, in the San Juan Islands. He fought on alone most of the time. I wished then, and still do, that I could have been with him.

Those medical records also told me that he was an alcoholic, that he'd had various conditions from something as simple as a deviated septum to syphilis (see, he was a bad boy) when he was younger. Unfortunately, there was not one word about any neurological diseases. He'd apparently had seizures several times, but the doctors thought that those were related to his alcoholism. And, seizures are not the same as tremors. They don't have the same causal factors, and generally emanate from different parts of the brain. Perhaps he had so many other problems that a tremor was never noticed, he'd never developed one, or he just never had my problem.

Did his parents have familial tremor? Maybe it skipped a generation? I still don't know if that's the case. A year or so later, I found Barbara, a Latham cousin on my paternal grandfather's side on Ancestry. She knew his family well and didn't think anyone had ever had that problem. I was still stuck.

Chapter Eleven

Two Disasters and Another Discovery

*"There's no disaster that can't become a blessing,
and no blessing that can't become a disaster."*
RICHARD BACH

By the early part of the new century, David and I had lived in Houston for slightly more than twenty years, and only had one experience with severe weather. We were told that we were lucky and were probably living on borrowed time. We were also told that if you hadn't been born in Texas, you had to live here for twenty years before you could say you were a Texan. So, I guess we're now Texans, y'all.

Our first brush with severe Texas weather was Tropical Storm Allison in 2001. In a period of six days, she dumped over thirty-five inches of rain on southeast Texas. That storm moved in and just hovered ominously over Houston. There were no fronts to push or pull it through. This behavior is called stalling. Weather stalling is much worse than people who drag their feet, something that drives me crazy. I learned to dislike weather stalling even more.

We watched all night as the water inundated our street. Allison flooded major highways and for days afterward made getting anywhere in Houston more of a nightmare than the usual snarled traffic is. That storm taught us that we were fortunate. We learned that our home was on the high spot on the street. Our nearby neighbors weren't quite so lucky. Houses next to and across the street from us flooded, leaving their occupants with standing water in their homes, which was soon followed by mold and mildew. Clean up and remediation service companies made a fortune, and many homeowners got new drywall, fresh paint, new carpeting, and new furniture they hadn't thought they'd need.

Dale, our first and only grandchild at the time, stayed with us the night Allison inundated Houston. I'll never forget watching him sleep peacefully while that storm raged on and on and on. It takes a lot to disturb the sleep of a busy, active, two-year-old.

David said, "I wish we could sleep like that, but I'm afraid of that water rising any higher."

That tropical storm hit Houston when I still thought I was an only child, and prior to my tremor diagnosis. David and I dealt with it alone, both that night, and after Allison eventually passed through. We were up all night, alternating between watching Dale and keeping an eye on the storm and the rising water. It rose to within a half inch of our front door.

At one point, I told David, "Good grief! We have trash bags floating down our street. Maybe we should try to put up some kind of barrier in front of the doors?"

"Good idea," he agreed. "Let's try to find something that might block the water."

Since we've never owned sand bags, we did the next best thing—we used a trash can to prop up some old folding doors that had been gathering dust in our garage.

They turned out to be perfect and gave David the hoarder a chance to tell me, "See, you never know when you might need something you think is useless."

Our high spot on the block, plus this hastily erected barrier, provided us with a narrow escape. Personal photo.

A scene after Allison moved on, along Highway 59 in Houston. By Houston/Galveston National Weather Service— http://www.srh.noaa.gov/hgx/projects/allison01/damagepictu res/hazard59_4.jpg, Public Domain, https://commons.wikimedia.org/w/index.php?curid=854507

Neither of us had experienced storms like that in Pennsylvania as were growing up, so we didn't know how to behave or what to do.

Our next encounter with tropical weather was Hurricane Ike, which hit in 2008. By this time, I knew I had an older half-sister. And I was working hard to solve that medical mystery. Allison was bad. Ike was quite another story. It was our first hurricane, since we'd moved to Houston after Alicia came roaring through in 1982, so we had no idea what to expect. Ike moved over Houston in the middle of the night, the scariest time, since we couldn't see what was going on outside very well. Driving rain that was nearly horizontal and no electricity made it difficult to see much of anything. Neither of us had any desire to venture out. We didn't care if we could say we'd experienced a hurricane up close and personal like the people on The Weather Channel do with some regularity. In spite of not being in the midst of the storm, we could hear the howling winds. I never want to hear winds like that again. We laid in bed listening to the thumps of tree limbs falling on our roof, hoping that they wouldn't break through.

At one point, I heard the telltale sound of a tornado. People say they sound like a train, and I can tell you firsthand that they do. I heard that roar, and my whole body started trembling. I couldn't decide if it was as scary as the symptoms of familial tremor—before I knew what was causing them—or not knowing what that tornado might do to us. I kept seeing images in my mind of storm destruction in Oklahoma, and I knew I didn't want to experience that.

When I heard that rumbling, my heart rate went bounding up.

I shook David, "Get out of bed! Now!"

He sat bolt upright, "Are you all right?"

I shrieked, "I'm fine, but I thought I heard a tornado. We need to get into the hallway. NOW!"

To this day, I am amazed how he could possibly have fallen asleep while that storm was raging. I guess he figured we two grownups could handle it, unlike Allison, when we were up all night, worrying that we'd have to evacuate with our two-year old grandson. Once I got him up, we hid in an inside hallway, as far away from windows as possible. On top of my usual tremors, I was shaking like the leaves on our trees.

We were lucky once again. Even with five very large, very old trees surrounding our house, the worst damage we had was a chain link fence that was bent away from its foundation. That fence caught and stopped a tulip tree from going through a new bay window we'd just had installed. So, we didn't mind having the fence damaged. In fact, I never liked that fence anyway.

At the time, we were living in an old ranch-style home that was erected on what was originally farmland. It was built in 1952. Three of our five large trees were Arizona Ash, which we were told have a lifespan of thirty years. Even though ours were healthy, trimmed, and well cared for, we worried about them. They were living on borrowed time.

Dalton, our seasoned "tree man," came out after the storm to clean up the trees and clear away the mess Ike left. He looked around the neighborhood, and without being prompted, said, "You had a tornado come through here. I can tell that from the damage to the trees. If you look, you can see the exact path it took."

I smugly told David, "See, I was right. Good thing we hid in that hallway."

He just said, "Harrumph," and shot me the fisheye he reserves for those times when I'm right and he's wrong.

Not everyone was as fortunate as we were. Ike created a powerful storm surge that wiped out nearly every home on the Bolivar Peninsula, on the upper

One of three giant Arizona Ash limbs that hit our house—thankfully, it didn't go through the roof. This one fell right over our bedroom. Personal photo.

Texas coast. It looked like a ghost town. That hurricane devastated Galveston. It broke windows in downtown Houston. We lost power, along with tens of thousands of other Houstonians, and were without it for two weeks. It was September, and it was hot and humid.

Even with no power, David and I managed well. We have a friend who has a business, and he maintained an apartment for one of his employees. That person just happened to be out of the country at the time, so after a few days, we moved in. There was electricity, there was air conditioning. There was even cable. Although it wasn't home, we were grateful to be there. Our friend shared his office with me, so I was even able to work. We learned to be thankful for the small things, like the City of Houston picking up our trash. We had a neighborhood eat-in in our front yard. We still have yearly Ike picnics. A hurricane like that is not something you forget. But, if you can associate something good with it, like a good friend who offers you a place to stay, and some good food with neighbors, it makes it harder to remember the bad parts.

My reactions to those two storms were quite different. During Allison, David and I were a team working alone. At that point, I thought I was an only child. After Ike, I knew I had an older half-sister. Following our first hurricane, David and I were part of a community, helping neighbors move tree limbs out of the streets. We formed work teams to help other neighbors clear away their debris.

One day when we were at the house, before the tree limbs had been removed, we heard thumping on the roof. We went outside to find our neighbor, a reconstructive surgeon, perched up there, getting rid of some of the debris. This is a man who makes his living with his hands, doing incredibly precise things. In spite of that, there he was sawing away.

When we asked him what on earth he was doing, he laughed his signature laugh that sounds like a cross between a donkey braying and an out-of-tune flugelhorn, and said, grinning, "I was bored."

We shared stories and freezer food in a big eating orgy with neighbors so we didn't have to throw it away. I learned to be part of something bigger than myself. My attitude shifted, just like the winds before and after the hurricane passed through. I had a sister. A family. Living through those two storms made me realize what a differ-ence finding family had done for me.

Eventually some linemen from Mississippi came through and restored our power. Along with our neigh-bors, we ran outside and cheered them when we saw their trucks. After a few weeks, we moved back home again.

Once the kerfuffle from the hurricane settled down, and several months after contacting my older half-sister,

Carolyn, I went back to my father's service records again. In the meantime, I'd stayed busy working and simply absorbing the fact that I wasn't an only child. It was a lot to process, and I completely understood Carolyn's "Oh" responses when we'd talked.

David was pleased at my discoveries, and nearly as excited, "I know how much this means to you, and I'm delighted that you've found a family after all these years. Maybe someday, you'll even get that medical mystery solved."

I saw in our father's Naval records that there were more children—a younger sister and a younger brother. It wasn't just Carolyn and me. Now we were four. Beyond being thrilled at finding more family, my hopes were raised for finding some medical information.

Chapter Twelve

A Younger Sister Finds Me

"I used to think I was the strangest person in the world but then I thought, there are so many people in the world, there must be someone just like me who feels bizarre and flawed in the same ways I do. I would imagine her and imagine that she must be out there thinking of me too. well, I hope that if you are out there you read this and know that yes, it's true I'm here, and I'm just as strange as you."
REBECCA KATHERINE MARTIN

Between getting to know Carolyn and dealing with Ike, I had been posting on Ancestry.com bulletin boards in the hope that there might be someone who used the site who knew something about my Lathams from Kentucky. Unbeknownst to me, that younger sister had been working on her own family tree on Ancestry. Apparently, while we were escapees from the storm, she saw my posting. She managed to find our telephone number and tried calling me. Neither she nor we realized that without power, there's no answering machine, so the phone just rang and rang and rang.

She later told me she thought, "What kind of people are these anyway? They don't even have an answering machine?" She lived in California, and never considered that pesky hurricane. So, she tried the next best thing—she wrote to me using my email address from Ancestry.com.

Once our power was restored, we moved back into our home late on a Friday evening. David got our internet connection going again. I decided that the world could wait a day for me to reappear. I was just glad to be home and looking forward to being back in our own bed again. I was mentally exhausted.

Just as I was drifting off to sleep, David yelled, "You got an email from your sister Liz!"

I just lay there in my near stupor, and thought, *who is he talking about?* Those service records referred to her as Elizabeth, not Liz.

I said groggily, "I'm tired; I'll deal with it in the morning." And promptly went to sleep.

The next morning, I was alert enough to realize what was going on.

I read her email and said, "Yes, that's my younger sister! She found me on Ancestry."

Liz left her full name and phone number and wrote, "Please call me!"

Of course, I did, as soon as the two-hour time difference between Houston and California allowed me to try to contact her at a respectable time. This call turned out to be much easier than the one I'd made to Carolyn. At least she was somewhat prepared, and I didn't think I'd have to worry about her falling over from shock.

We talked for two and a half hours. As strained as the conversation with Carolyn was, this was like reconnecting with an old friend. We laughed and tried to cram a lifetime of experiences into one telephone conversation. We had a grand time sharing stories and starting to get to know one another.

It turned out that we had similar career backgrounds, both of us spending time in corporate America. Liz and I were making our ways at a time when there weren't many women in management jobs. We talked about our work experiences, our spouses, our kids, and our grandkids. Liz told me a little bit about her brother, Eddie. I now had two half-sisters and a half-brother, plus a collection of nieces and nephews. Two nephews from Carolyn, two nephews from Liz, and three nieces from Eddie.

David just sat and listened, with a big grin on his face.

After we wrapped up our call, he said, "Good grief, she's as bad as you are!"

He meant talking. We would later discover that we had many more similarities than just telephone yakking (as David calls it).

Disappointingly, like Carolyn, Liz had no idea about our father's medical history. She was nine years old when her mother divorced him, and she never knew any of his family either. I'd hit another medical dead-end. By this time, I'd come to the realization that I'd likely never find out. I accepted that, and instead focused on finding and establishing ties with family. Best of all, it was clear that I was connecting with my own big family.

Chapter Thirteen

Are There Any More Like Us Out There? Turns Out There Are!

"Then you're really in for a big surprise."
SARAH J. MAAS

During our conversations, Liz and I talked about our Dad's Navy career. It was a long one, at twenty years, and we decided that he must have been the classic sailor, with a girl in every port. Maybe more. It seems that he was a bit of a bad boy, which I'd learned in reading some of his Navy disciplinary records. He was cited for being AOL (absent over leave) numerous times. Some of those AOLs were instances where he'd leave the ship or base, and spend it somewhere else, rather than with Carolyn and her mother, Ethel. Then he'd return to his station late. I learned from Liz that some of those occasions were meetings between him and the woman who would subsequently become Liz's and Ed's mother. More on that later. In addition, Carolyn had told me that her mother became totally disgusted with his behavior, and that's what led to their divorce.

Liz posed a perfectly logical question. "I wonder how many others there might be besides the four of us?"

Laughing, I chimed in, "Who knows? I can't help but think there's probably a good chance of finding more."

We chortled and snickered and thought at the time that was very funny.

Ike's September madness, with its heat and humidity, morphed into October, and the weather started becoming more bearable in Houston. We could even stand to go outside for brief periods.

Then, one afternoon, I got a call from Liz. I remember it vividly, standing in the kitchen, talking on our landline phone.

She said, excitedly, "You are not going to believe this! We were right. There's another one."

I just chuckled and said, "Well, he *was* a sailor. How did you find this out? There weren't any more children listed in his Naval records."

It turned out that our postings on Ancestry had gotten some attention from somebody else—the daughter of yet another Latham child. She called her dad with the news, and he called Liz, whose phone number was on that Ancestry bulletin board.

Now we were five. I gained a big brother, Ted, and discovered that I am the middle child. Ted's daughter, Karen, who found Liz on Ancestry, lives in Seattle. And, Ted has another daughter, Amelia, who lives about twenty miles from Liz, in northern California. He told Liz that he and his wife were planning a trip there after Thanksgiving.

I told David: "For years, I have been spending time with your family. Now it's my turn. We're going to California the weekend after Thanksgiving."

He was tickled pink, and as eager as I was to meet some of my newly-found siblings. We cashed in some frequent flyer miles, and off we went. Meanwhile, I'd had several conversations with Ted, and we were all excited about meeting up.

Our son, meanwhile, wasn't quite so thrilled. His mother was going off to California to meet a bunch of people that she'd met on the internet. None of us knew them, and he didn't like it one little bit.

He told his wife, "These people could be axe murderers for all we know."

He didn't tell us that. His wife, Trish, did. We still laugh about it. It was the hit of our meetup.

Chapter Fourteen

Revelations in a Hotel Lobby

*"It seemed like a joke, how much all of
these dudes looked alike..."*
GILLIAN FLYNN

Thanksgiving 2008 finally came, following weeks of
pent-up anticipation and anxiety about meeting my new
family. Except for hiding in a hallway from the tornado
during Hurricane Ike, I don't think time had ever passed
more slowly for me. That twister seemed to take forever
to pass, and I couldn't wait to take off for California. My
bags were packed two weeks before we left.

I'd spoken to both Liz and Ted on the phone numerous
times, and we'd shared some family photographs and
stories, but it wasn't like actually being in the same room
at the same time. This meeting would allow us to look
into each other's eyes and actually touch one another. It
suddenly became much more real. We'd invited Carolyn,
who did not join us—she wasn't much of a traveler. Liz
was still estranged from Eddie at that time, so it was just
Liz, Ted, and I. Three of the then-known five.

Because we were all novices at this game (who wouldn't
be?), we decided it might be best to meet initially on
some neutral ground. Ted and his wife had been in the

area many times near where Liz lived since one of his daughters and her two daughters lived nearby. He suggested a hotel where they'd stayed many times that was convenient, comfortable, and economical. Not knowing what other alternatives might be better, and since the hotel got pretty good reviews online, David and I made reservations there. We planned for Liz and her husband, Ron, to come over and meet us all there.

Our flight got into Sacramento on time and our luggage actually arrived with us. The car rental process went smoothly, with no problems, so we took all these as good signs that our meeting would be successful. We gathered up our baggage and set off for the big meeting. The weather was beautiful, with clear blue skies, and cool, but not cold, temperatures. Exactly what California weather should be. Thanks to GPS—a godsend for people like me with no sense of direction—it was an easy trip. Ted's hotel suggestion turned out to be just fine. At least for David and me.

I have always loved California and have teased David for years about how lucky he was to get a "California girl." Having found family and discovering that they were all Californians (or had been for long periods of their lives), I suspected that there might be more to it than the fact that I was born there.

Sacramento was no exception to my "California rule" of feeling as if I were home again. I'd spent time either for business or on personal trips in LA, San Francisco, San Diego, Napa Valley, and even the not-very-exciting farming community of Bakersfield. I'd never been to Sacramento or the northern part of the state. Once I arrived, I felt that I'd come back to where I belonged. It's hard to describe, but on every occasion I'd been in the state, I had that sensation. Only on this trip, I had a better idea why.

When the time came to meet, David and I went to the lobby. I fidgeted nervously, as David tried to calm me. Then Ted and his wife, Virginia, came in. As good as our hotel experience was, Ted's and Virginia's was equally bad.

Ted looked obviously upset and told us, "I cannot believe it, but we have ants in our room, and are having trouble getting the management to move us into an ant-free room. We've never had such a negative experience like this here. I feel really horrible about recommending this place to you. Are you guys having any problems?"

"Please, don't worry about it," I told him. "Our room is fine, and we don't think you made a bad choice. We do think you should demand that the management get you moved."

Fortunately, he did that and eventually they got an antless room.

Poor Ted's biggest anxiety wasn't that he was having problems. He was concerned we might have a similar problem. He was overly worried about this since he'd recommended the place. It was then that I learned what a caring, empathetic person he is. He was more anxious about us and our reactions than he was about his own negative experience. That was the beginning of my realization that I'd gotten a really terrific big brother. I wish he'd been around when I was a kid. He would have protected me from bullies and tears along the way.

We had just barely started comparing travel notes when Liz and Ron came in. Although we three had pictures of each other, it was amazing to actually meet two people with a genetic connection who had so many physical similarities to me. We had the same noses, curly hair, high foreheads, and remarkably comparable smiles. That's when the fun began.

Our first meeting started off with lots of hugs. That's what you do when you're family, right? When I was a kid growing up, my mother's family was not very demonstrative. We were not big huggers. Fortunately, living in Texas taught me that my childhood might not have been the norm. In Texas, and throughout the South, *everybody* hugs everybody else. Even my clients hugged me. So, the embraces felt normal and natural. In my life, it seems like every experience prepared me for another. That was certainly true in this case. Our hugging felt better than I could have imagined. I had waited sixty-two years for it.

We began with innocuous questions about travel and the hotel until we began to feel more comfortable. Then we moved on to physical appearances. The first thing we noticed was that Ted is quite tall, over six feet.

Liz and I said, almost simultaneously, "Wow, you are really tall!"

We then looked at each other and decided that we are on the shrimpy side.

I explained, "My mom was very short, five feet, one and a half inches tall, so I come by it honestly."

Liz offered, "My mother was short too."

I told them, "I learned from our dad's Naval records that he was not a big man either. He grew from five feet six inches when he enlisted in the Navy to about five feet nine inches when he reached his full adulthood."

Liz and I both made some obvious silly comments about where Ted got his height that involved milkmen and other assorted non-related males. When you're in a situation where you've just discovered a completely new family, especially one with one father and the four different mothers we knew about at that time, acceptance and humor are good traits to have. Fortunately, we all had them, including our spouses, who were enjoying themselves as much as we siblings were with this unique situation.

We moved past height and on to other physical characteristics. We quickly saw that we all have very high foreheads.

Liz said, "I guess that old wives' tale about people with high foreheads being highly intelligent must be true. After all, we're living proof!"

I added, "Of course, and, apparently, our Dad had a high forehead, too."

Then we proceeded down to noses. Liz, Ted, and I had the same noses. When I was a kid, I could never understand why my nose wasn't pretty like my Mom's. Hers was little and pert. Mine is long, with a bump that comes in handy to hold my glasses up. Functional, but I consider it unattractive. Now I understood. Besides the possibility of that familial tremor, I inherited a Latham nose. And, inside that nose, a deviated septum, just like my dad's.

Next was hair.

I told my half-siblings, "As a child, I had curly, frizzy hair that no one else in my mother's family had. I hated it. My mother, by contrast, thought it was beautiful. I would sit and squirm, while she would tell me how beautiful it was and how she loved playing with all those tiny little ringlets."

Liz said, "I know, I had the same issue. If we'd had beautiful, smooth Shirley Temple curls, it would have been okay. But we had frizz too, didn't we?"

To Liz and me, those beautiful little curls were just one more thing that made us different. We all know that kids never want to be different. For me, it was almost a pathological reaction. It was just one more thing that made me unlike other kids, and I always wanted to be like the other kids. Especially the "cool kids." I tried all kinds of things to make my hair look more "normal," like constantly sleeping on giant rollers to try to straighten it out some- what. It worked fine until the Philadelphia humidity got to it. Then, poof, the frizzies set in again. Ted was luckier. He had short boy hair, so his curls were camouflaged.

At our meetup, we discovered that I was not the only one with that kind of hair. Later, we found out that both of Ted's daughters had hair just like mine had been when I was a child. At last, I finally knew where those miserable curls came from. Apparently, I passed that gene on to my son Mike, and he passed it on to his son, Dale, and his daughter, Elise. Mike had an Afro when he was in high school that was the envy of the Black kids. So, my father's "curl" legacy goes on. I hope to live long enough to meet our grandchildren's children to see if they get the curls, too. I'm betting they will.

Mike, starting to work on his "Fro."
It got bigger. Much bigger. Personal photo.

During our meetup, we talked about our mothers, and made a number of interesting discoveries. All of them had been brunettes, so, unlike the Broadway musical, *Gentlemen Prefer Blondes*, apparently, our Dad did not have a preference for women with light hair. Since he likely would not have been considered a gentleman, we all decided that was a perfect fit.

We also began to realize just how little the mothers talked about our shared Dad. Generally, they said little to nothing, under any circumstances, even when asked. It wasn't just my mom. It was Liz and Ted's mothers, too. In my conversations with Carolyn, she told me the same thing. I suspected that put the final nail in the coffin of my finding out my father's full medical history. None of us siblings knew very much about the man at all. We did know about the mothers, though. Hearing and comparing their stories was fascinating.

From physical similarities, we talked about careers and what we'd done with our lives up until that point. Ted had been in the Army and moved on from that to law enforcement. He told us a few funny cop stories. I'm sure over the years we'll continue to hear more. The best was one of how he'd talked down a man with a knife that several other cops couldn't subdue with force.

Ted told us, "I simply talked to him quietly and convinced him that he didn't want me to have to put him in the hospital. The nurses were mean there, and the jail was a much nicer place, with better food."

It worked, and the criminal backed down. Ted had the height and the bulk to be convincing that he could seriously and easily harm the fellow. That story illuminated his personality as much as those of the perps he'd encountered. Probably more so. Once again, I realized what a terrific big brother I'd found. He could protect me from bad guys and do it in a humane and thoughtful fashion. This was real life; better than a TV cop drama.

Liz and I talked in more detail about our middle-management careers in corporate America. She had a life-long stint with AT&T, and I had two shorter corporate gigs: one at Owens-Illinois in Toledo, Ohio; and one at Baker Hughes in Houston. It turned out that we were both early pioneers in that game. We shared many war stories that were of the same genre and eras. Of course, we were both paid less than our male counterparts, a situation that irritated us immensely. Liz and I are disappointed that it is not significantly better now for women than it was in the 1970s. In spite of that, we also laughed a lot about the ridiculous situations that trailblazers like us had to put up with. When I first started working after getting my MBA in 1975, my company had a strict policy against women wearing pants, even pantsuits, to work. Hillary Clinton would have hated it. It's funny now, but was very grating then when pantsuits were becoming fashionable. Not to mention practical in cold Toledo winters.

We talked about our kids, and their kids, and how they had changed our lives. Carolyn, Ted, and Liz all had multiple children, while David and I had just one. In addition, with one exception, the "girls" had boy children, while the "boys" had girls. I shared some of our funny stories, like Mike getting the measles the day we were leaving on a vacation. Since he felt fine, and kids are not contagious after they break out, we just slathered him over with Calamine lotion and went anyway. On that same trip, we discovered our dog couldn't swim. David had to rescue him from drowning. Poor old Maxie was a city dog. He thought that water only came in puddles that he could walk through.

Liz remarked, "I can't wait to tell my sons about our meeting and share some of your stories."

"I know," I replied, "Mike and Trish are anxious to hear about it too. Maybe they'll eventually get over being jealous."

Liz agreed, "Mine feel the same way too. Hopefully, some stories will soothe their bruised egos a bit."

After we got home without being chopped into little pieces by those potential axe murderers, Mike & Trish admitted that they wished they'd been included.

During our first meeting, Ted, Liz, and I did most of the talking, so our respective spouses were pretty quiet. Not that we gave them much of a chance. Ted tends to be quieter than Liz or me, but he held his own. We three dominated the conversation. Usually, most people wouldn't stand a chance against just Liz and me.

Despite our incessant talking, that didn't mean that those spouses weren't listening and watching. Ron, David, and Virginia sat in rapt attention, smiling constantly and thoroughly enjoying the spectacle. Not only did we notice the many similarities between us, but our spouses also did. The funniest example of this was my husband, David, who sat and looked like someone at a tennis match, since I was on his left side and Liz on his right. I'm sure his neck was getting sore.

Finally, he said, "You know, there were times when I wasn't sure who was talking. You two not only look a lot alike, but your mannerisms are the same! How could that be when you didn't even grow up together? It's spooky."

Liz, Ted, and I laughed, and I said, "I guess that genetics stuff is really true."

We all shared how weird we felt as kids, being different

than our friends. Even Liz and Eddie, who had a full-time dad until Liz was nine and Eddie was seven, felt that way. None of us had a father in our formative years. Most of our friends did. Throughout our childhoods, we weren't sure why we were different and didn't have a father to protect and care for us.

We had vastly different home lives growing up in the 1950s than The Beaver or Ricky and David Nelson. None of us had two parents, except for a short stretch for Liz and Eddie. All of us had only one—a mom—for most of our young lives.

Liz pointed out, "You know, life for us in the 1950s was very different than the Cleavers and Ozzie and Harriet."

Ted agreed, "On top of that, we had mothers that would never talk about our father."

I added, "Carolyn has told me that she felt the same way we three did as a child. Weird. And, her mom would never talk about our father either."

To us as kids, that meant something was terribly wrong. Of course, we thought it was something the matter with us. It had to be our fault. Carolyn, Ted, and I didn't have any siblings, so we didn't even have a conspirator to share those feelings with. And this was not something you'd share with a friend. Even a best friend. Liz had Eddie, but she mostly ignored him growing up. Beyond the fact that she thought he was a stupid boy, he was sickly as a kid, so that didn't help. In addition, it allowed him to get away with murder with their mom. When he made her mad, Liz got even by making him wear a dress to the grocery store when her mom told her to get him ready to go. Like all sisters' attitudes toward their little brothers, she thought he was a pest.

We dominated that hotel lobby for hours, and our laughter and stories caused a bit of a stir among the front desk staff, who were fascinated and enveloped in smiles once they realized what we were engaged in. And other guests, who came and went during our meeting, gave us curious glances, and then huge grins when they caught on to what was going on. The Latham Show was a good start.

Chapter Fifteen

The Beginnings of Family

"Family is not an important thing. It's everything."
MICHAEL J. FOX

Our hotel lobby meeting went so well that we all decided to keep up the momentum. Liz invited us over for dinner that evening, and we included one of Ted's daughters and one of her daughters. That really fueled the jealousy fires among the other children of the siblings. They all later admitted that they didn't understand why they weren't included when one of Ted's daughters was. We told them that they weren't excluded, but Alice and Renee were included because of geography, since they lived so close. They understood, and were somewhat mollified, but it still left them smarting.

We discovered that Liz is a great cook, and that she and Ron like wine, so we had a perfect environment. She made a tri-tip roast, which apparently is a California thing. David and I had never heard of it. It was delicious, tender, well-seasoned, and succulent. She served it with creamy mashed potatoes and green beans. Yum. You can buy tri-tip roasts now in Texas. In 2008, they were a novelty for us.

Once again, we started with big hugs and had no lack of things to talk about. After all, we had to make up for years of not knowing each other and our stories. It was a wonderful, noisy, laughter-filled evening.

Mary Jo and Liz. Personal photo

Ted's daughter Alice, of the super-curly hair fame, and Renee came to the same realizations we had about looks, high foreheads, and temperaments. That day held a lot of "oh, wow" moments as we made each discovery of physical similarities. We tried catching them up on some of the things we had talked about, so it was a somewhat boisterous gathering. Even the spouses got into it, since they had stories from our hotel lobby meeting that they wanted to tell. We were so anxious to share, that there were times when Liz, Ted, and I started talking at once, to be joined by the spouses, then laughed as we caught ourselves. Alice and Renee quietly watched us and smiled. I suspect their cheeks were sore by the end of the evening. I told the axe murderer story to the delight of everyone. Of course, the wine didn't hurt the atmosphere of general merriment. It was like an early Christmas. For me, that trip was the best gift I had ever received.

I had been collecting as many photographs as I could of

our Dad and our mothers and brought my laptop along so I could share all of them with everyone. I had some photos of our paternal grandparents and some of our dad that Carolyn had shared with me. Once again, I realized how lucky we were to have technical advances on our side. This story could never have happened even twenty years ago. Thanks to DNA and genealogy, people finding family they never knew about has been happening more frequently. Hopefully, most of their experiences have been as positive as ours.

When I returned home, I set up a family website on *myfamily.com*, and we all contributed more photographs and shared our birthdays and anniversaries. After all, this was new to us, and we had a lot to learn about each other. Unfortunately, this site was acquired by Ancestry.com and they shut it down in September 2014. Nevertheless, by that time, we all had the same information, since I shared our Dad's service records and his Navy medical records with my new half-sisters and half-brothers. My genealogy work on Ancestry.com came in handy, and I've added substantially to a giant family tree that now includes the siblings' families.

I told stories of my Mom's journey in the Marine Corps during World War II. Liz told some about her Mom's migration from Texas to California. Ted's stories were the most interesting. Later chapters will reveal their stories, as well as our father's. We decided that our journey and those histories couldn't die with us. They must be preserved.

While we were in California, we had time to spend with each other individually. We had a great trip to a gold mine in a state park and enjoyed several other meals with Liz and her husband Ron. We saw some of Sacramento with

Ted and his wife. That made it easier for us to get to know each other on more of a one-on-one basis. In none of those meetings were we uncomfortable or lacked for things to talk about. For me, there was no stress. It was like coming back to a long-lost home I never knew I had.

———◦◦———

Time ticked on. Carolyn, Liz, Ted and I stayed in touch. Carolyn by letter or phone, Liz, Ted, and I by phone and email. At this point, Liz and Eddie were totally estranged, and she told me that they hadn't spoken for years.

It was only much later, on his 60th birthday in 2013, that I had the chance to get to know him. In Las Vegas, no less. As with many things in my new-found family, there's a funny story behind that. Apparently, besides being as quiet as Liz and I are talkative, Eddie is not a gambler, but one of his daughters loves Las Vegas. She told him they were taking him there for his birthday. Evidently, it didn't matter to her that her dad didn't care about gambling and cared even less about going to Vegas; they were going there anyway.

What she didn't tell him was that Liz and her husband, Ron, and David and I would be there too. The five of us spent a minimal amount of time in the casinos and had an obligatory buffet in one of them. Instead, we went to Red Rock Canyon, Hoover Dam, and The Mob Museum. All of them were much more interesting than spending an entire day in front of noisy slot machines. It was the beginning of a reunification between Liz and Eddie, which gave me a good feeling. Had I not started on my family medical history quest, I'm not sure that would have happened. Our trip gave me an opportunity to get to know my baby brother, and we spent the weekend talking and laughing, and sharing stories. The daughter that instigated this trip spent all of her time in the casinos, of course.

While we were all playing tourists in Nevada, we went to a restaurant for lunch and were standing together to pay on the way out. Liz, Eddie and I were chatting, while David and Ron settled the bill. The cashier stopped right in the middle of her duties, and looked up at us wide-eyed, saying, "Well, you three certainly can't deny that you're related!" We laughed at that, but it gave me a warm, satisfying feeling to be recognized as part of my new family.

Mary Jo, Eddie, and Liz. Personal photo.

Chapter Sixteen

A Final (?) Discovery

"No one is so brave that he is not disturbed by something unexpected."
JULIUS CAESAR

After our siblings' meetup in late 2008, I went back to work and Liz and Ted returned to their lives. We stayed in touch and continued to wonder if there were any more Latham children lurking out there. I suspect we will always question that. Life happened. Three years passed, more quickly than years used to.

———⟐———

Skip ahead to January 2012. My husband, David, decided he'd had enough fun working. He came home one day, visibly upset, and said, "I've had enough. I'm retiring. I can't stand the BS that's going on at work. We can handle it financially, and if I don't stop now, heaven knows what kind of a toll it will take on me."

Knowing our financial situation was stable, I urged him on, "I don't know how you've kept at it this long. I know you wanted to max out on Social Security in two years, when you reached seventy. But, you're right, staying would likely ruin your health, or even kill you. Besides, I have no intention of quitting yet, so I'll still be bringing in some money. Eventually, I'll get to the max point with Social Security, in two to four years, when I hit sixty-eight or seventy, then I'll quit too."

Now I had a full-time business as well as a full-time husband, who was in my office during my working hours. I was used to sharing that office with our dog, Riley, and the occasional Houston mosquito. Riley was a great office companion, very quiet, and only interrupted me when nature called. The atmosphere in our shared office, once David retired, was tense at times.

I was so used to being alone in my little working world that I would forget David was occupying part of my space. This really wasn't a problem.

Until the interruptions began.

Busily squirreling away on an analysis of some data or putting together a PowerPoint presentation, I'd hear, "You would not believe what I just read!"

"No," I snipped, "and what's more, I'd really rather not hear it at this very instant."

Of course, that made him feel bad, so I'd have to say, "I'm sorry, I'm right in the middle of something. Can we talk about this over dinner?"

That helped his bruised ego a bit, but he'd sulk for a while just to show me how "mean" I was. After a number of discussions, we somehow managed to come to a meeting of the minds without annoying each other too much. He continued working on genealogy and kept an eye on the stock market, while I probed the minds of customers for my clients.

Now we're both retired, he thinks I interrupt him. Turnabout is fair play, I suppose. Or perhaps it's me getting revenge.

Meanwhile, I began to plan for my ultimate retirement and started working with a fellow market researcher.

Susan and I thought a lot alike, and she ran her business as I ran mine. We met often to discuss my clients and what steps we'd need to take to transition my business over to hers. Many times, we'd get together over lunch, usually at one of the many trendy Houston restaurants "inside the Loop," the designation for those neighborhoods that are within the boundaries of the 610 Loop, which circles Houston. We both firmly believed that there was nothing wrong with enjoying yourself while you do business.

I cut back on my new business activities, which gave me more free time, hoping that would help me ease into retirement rather than being plunged into it like a dip in freezing water. I didn't want to have a hard stop that would leave me at an end point in my life with nothing left to do. That happens to too many people when they retire, and I was determined not to be one of them. I stayed as busy as I wanted to be and felt pleased with myself for managing things so well. Our timeframe was two years for a complete handover.

In December 2012, David and I learned about *23andMe*, a company that offers personal genetic testing to help you solve ancestral mysteries, tell you where your forebears came from, and explain the genetic traits that could have an impact on your health. They also encourage users to complete short surveys that ask about medical conditions and food preferences. If you agree to it, they share your data (without personal information, of course) to researchers who are investigating diseases and genetic traits. The genetic data, plus your answers to their survey questions, have yielded a wealth of information on inherited diseases, and may make "personalized medicine" a reality. Best of all, they show how your chromosomes match with others who have also done their testing.

Of course, David and I knew we just had to do it. We sent off our money and waited excitedly for our kits.

When they arrived, David shot me a wicked look as we spit into our tubes. "Wouldn't it be funny if this testing turns up more Lathams?"

"Ha ha," I snorted. "Maybe we can start a pool for the total number of kids. We're now up to five, and we haven't even considered investigating in Guam. Seriously, though, if they know some family medical history, I don't care how many we are."

Like the *Genographic* project, we mailed in our samples, and waited for the results. After less time than it took for the Navy to send my father's records, we got our results back. *23andMe* has a well-designed, interactive website where you can review all they've found out about you. Our ancestries looked like what we had expected—mostly European. Surprisingly, mine contained a small, but significant, according to geneticists, percentage of Sub-Saharan African genes, at about 0.6%. That percentage would mean that about seven or eight generations back, I had an ancestor who was full-blooded African. Apparently, this is not unusual for people with colonial American ancestry, which I knew I had. When my Black friends learn about this, they tell me they always knew there was a reason I was so cool.

Of course, I had to run down this rabbit hole. I told David, "I'd really like to be able to trace that root."

His reply was typical of David, "Of course you do. I know how you are. But, I suspect you may have some trouble doing it."

From genealogy and reading about what life was like in Colonial America, I had a feel for how those first colonists lived in the 1700s. I uncovered census data from that time period that indicated ancestors on both sides of my family owned slaves. So, this was not something I could pin on my Latham ancestors. It also made it less likely that I could narrow down exactly who it came from.

The early census reports tell a tale of how slaves—and women—were treated in that early stage of our country's history. Only men were identified by name, with wives and children shown only by number and gender. To the dismay of many a genealogist, those wives and children were not identified by name until the 1860 census. If there were slaves in the household, they too were counted as numbers of males, females, and children. Even the male slaves were not named. Slaves, wives, and children were recorded like property.

You may recall the publicity about Thomas Jefferson and his now-famous relationship with one of his slaves, Sally Hemmings. DNA testing on both Jefferson's and Hemming's descendants has since definitively proved that their relationship produced children. My small percentage of Sub-Saharan African means that someone in colonial times in my family must have had a relationship with someone with 100% African ancestry, most likely a slave (since there were more of them). Another possibly would be a free Black person. I assumed it was in my mother's family, since we had so many Colonists there. That theory may have been dashed, when Mary Lou, one of my first cousins on my mother's side, was tested. Her profile had zero African genes. Apparently, either she may not have gotten those genes, or they came from my father's side. It looked like I'd uncovered another Latham mystery.

When I looked at *23andMe*'s website, I found a boat-load of cousins, many of whom were third or fourth, with even more distant fifth and sixth. The website shows how strong the match is as a percentage of your chromosomes. People who they label as third and fourth cousins have a higher match rate than those who are fifth or sixth relatives. The site has an option for you to send a message to these people, who may or may not be willing to share their genetic makeup with you. If they do, you can see exactly which chromosomes the matches are on. I found many people on my mom's side, who mostly traced back to the Bakers, my grandfather's ancestors, and the Benckerts, my grandmother's. Although these "cousins" and I tried hard to find where our common ancestors were, most led to dead ends. While we shared common names, we couldn't find our common ancestors. Even with DNA data, genealogy is not easy.

My first cousin, Mary Lou, is also a genealogist. She is even more serious than David and I, and has found some interesting family history, like our third great grandfather, Samuel Phillippe, who was the inventor of the fly rod. Maybe that's why I like to fish. She and I have a high match rate, at eleven percent, and we could see on which parts of the chromosomes we matched. Very cool science. Knowing where those matches were would come in handy later.

David's 23andMe results were not as interesting as mine were. But he has a small amount (0.1%) of East Asian or Native American. Subsequent reporting shows that it's Yakut, Turkic people who inhabit the northeastern part of Russia. We have no idea where that might have come from, but it must be very old, at least nine or ten generations. When you read something like *Ancestral Journeys*, a book that details how Europe was populated, you get a better feel for how ancient peoples moved about.

We both got some insights into health issues, including the known inherited disorders we have and the likelihood that we might develop problems in our lifetimes. Their results nailed me on two traits that I knew I had, based on prior medical problems, and it was reassuring to have this verified. One of the traits they included was Familial Tremor. Although that one got my hopes up, their results indicated that I had only an average chance at developing this disease.

Life went on as normal, then September rolled around. I went for my usual yearly routine mammogram like a good girl and thought how nice it would be to not have to do that again for another year, until my Ob-Gyn's office called shortly after I got home.

The nurse told me, "Dr. Cook wants you to come in this afternoon."

"Why?" I asked, knowing in my heart that there was something in that mammogram that wasn't good.

"He'll talk to you when you come in."

While I realized that doctors' staffs cannot tell you anything, this just made me crazy. David and I hustled over to his office. Fortunately, it was close to home.

On the way, with a rock in the pit of my stomach the size of a small boulder, I told David, "You know this is not good. But with quality treatment and a positive attitude, we'll get through it."

He smiled a sad little smile, "I know, but that doesn't mean I won't worry."

When we arrived at Dr. Cook's office, we were ushered into a conference room, where we waited. And waited. And waited. Most women know that Ob-Gyns are not known for being prompt, and mine was very adept at it. I am not a patient person, especially when I know someone is going to tell me something bad.

I complained to David, while fidgeting, "Gee, you'd think he could at least not make us wait like this."

He agreed, trying to soothe me, "You're right, but I'm sure he's not doing it on purpose."

Dr. Cook finally came in, without his usual smiley face. He sat facing David and me, looking very serious and gloomy. He's normally a chatty, pleasant guy. On this day, he was all business, with a hint of worry.

He reached out for my shaky hand and told me, "There's no easy way to say this—you have breast cancer. The good news is that it appears to be contained, and you're here in Houston with one of the best cancer centers in the world. I can set you up with someone, if you like. There's a woman there who did a fellowship with me, and she's top notch."

David and I both started talking at once.

I finally said, "One of our neighbors is a reconstructive surgeon at MD Anderson. We'll talk to him before we choose someone to work with on this."

Dr. Cook reassured us, "Of course. This is not something that you have to rush into. And it's important that you find someone you're comfortable working with."

My cousin Mary Lou's mother died of breast cancer when I was about five years old. It was horrifying for the whole family to watch her go from healthy to failing in a short period of time. I remember thinking that it couldn't be possible for someone who looked so vibrant to be so sick. But she was. I suspect that she must have had a Stage 4 tumor that metastasized rapidly. That was in the early 1950s, before the good early detection and treatments we're lucky to have today.

My *23andMe* results showed that I was below average risk for breast cancer, and that I did not have a mutation on either the BRCA1 or BRCA2 gene. These gene mutations lead to an increased risk of developing breast cancer. I even shared this knowledge with the radiologist who did the biopsy, with Dr. Cook, and with my MD Anderson team. They all told me the same thing—not having those mutations did not guarantee you wouldn't get cancer. So much for that argument. Besides, there was no debating the fact that a lump showed up in that mammogram and a biopsy identified the abnormal cells.

Little did I know then, but when you become a patient at MD Anderson, you don't just get one doctor, you get a team of experts who guide you through your cancer journey. I started with a surgeon, then got a reconstructive surgeon, then added both a medical and a radiation oncologist. I was also given the option of consulting other professionals, like psychologists, nutritionists, and genetic counselors. In addition, there are many support groups that you can tap into. Throughout this journey, I've learned that cancer is not nearly as scary as it used to be, and that many patients I met along the way were in much worse shape than I was. I began to feel more optimistic.

I had two positive things going for me: the diagnosis was not horrific; and, at the time, we lived near the Texas Medical Center. Our next-door neighbor (the one who was sawing away at the branches on our roof after Hurricane Ike), was a reconstructive surgeon at MD Anderson, and his wife worked in the same department, as a Physician's Assistant. We were lucky to have two experts to depend on.

We all swung into action. I was quickly accepted as a patient, and teamed with Dr. Kelly Hunt, one of their top surgeons. I spent what I felt was an enormous amount of time at MD Anderson, having a battery of tests, followed by another biopsy, and was scheduled for surgery—a lumpectomy—in October. Our car learned the way there so well, we barely had to steer it. I was also paired with a perfectionist reconstructive surgeon (not our neighbor, of course), and he worked his magic. If you have to have a reconstructive surgeon, you want a perfectionist. I was worried, but I knew that I was in good hands. I had the A-team working on me.

Fortunately, like my neurological disease, this breast cancer diagnosis was not as bad as it could have been. I was lucky once again, getting the least bad thing.

My surgeon, Dr. Hunt, told me, "You have something called DCIS (Ductal Carcinoma in Situ), and it is Stage 0."

Until that time, I never knew there was a Stage 0.

I asked, "What does Stage 0 mean?"

She said, "It means it's good. Your cancer is fully encapsulated and is probably not invasive. A very, *very* good thing."

David was a wreck. It's always harder on the patient's other half. He hovered over me from the initial diagnosis until I was declared cancer-free in December 2015. He still hovers. So far, my top-notch cancer team and I have beat it. I now meet with the group at MD Anderson who specialize in survivorship. I'm now officially a survivor.

For five years after radiation, I will take Tamoxifen, a drug that lowers estrogen levels, since my tumor was estrogen-sensitive. It makes my skin as dry as a desert, thins my already sparse hair, and gives me nails that either crumble or tear, thanks to what little estrogen I had being nearly wiped out. I think that's a small price to pay for reducing my risk of cancer recurrence by half. I make up for it by slathering moisturizers and volumizers on my skin and hair and pop a high-dose biotin capsule every day to try to save what little is left of my nails.

After the surgery, I had radiation therapy for six weeks, five days a week, until early January 2014. Beyond being tedious—having to go every day—I knew it would kill off whatever nasty cancer cells might remain and sailed through it like a champ. I went through radiation during the holidays, from Thanksgiving 2013 through the new year of 2014. Being there with others going through the same thing helped, and I met some nice women on that part of my journey. It made me realize again just how lucky I was. Many of them were not only in worse medical shape, but also were far from home and their families. Since I still felt fine, I baked and brought cookies several times. There's nothing like a cookie to cheer you up.

My radiation oncologist, Dr. Strom, is a terrific guy. Like my neurologist, he has a great sense of humor, and we've spent many hours talking about vacations and the sometimes-funny things that happen on them. He tells us stories of his daughter, and David and I tell him about our grandchildren, Dale and Elise. Now that I'm in survivorship mode, I won't see him again. I'll miss him.

When he first began treating me, I told him about some of my earliest jobs, especially the time I spent in a nuclear medicine lab at a VA hospital.

He said, "That's cool, so I guess it wouldn't scare you to hear some of the more technical aspects of radiation therapy."

I replied, "Bring it on!"

I suspect he shared far more details with us on radiation therapy than he probably does with most patients.

MD Anderson has a tradition of ringing a bell when your treatments end. David and I were very happy when we got to ring that bell.

The bright side of this entire experience was I had one perky boob! Part of the lumpectomy included what's called a reduction and lift—performed by that perfectionist. The lift is basically a boob job that counteracts the effects of gravity that you experience after living so long. In March 2015, after the radiation effects had worn off and the tissue had stabilized, he did reconstructive work on the other side. I never would have dreamed that at the ripe old age of sixty-nine, I'd have that kind of cosmetic surgery. Of course, I've never had *any* cosmetic surgery, so this was a really big deal. Now I have two perky ones. Our daughter-in-law, Trish, is jealous that I don't have to wear a bra.

Even if cancer doesn't kill you, it has an impact on how you think about yourself and your future. I decided to move up my target retirement date, wanting to spend more time with my family and less time reacting to client demands. Financially, we were able to swing it, so in December 2013, I officially retired. My colleague, Susan, was ready and willing to take over, and our transition went very smoothly. As they say, PPPPPP—Prior Planning Prevents Piss-Poor Performance.

My cancer journey is just the backdrop that paved the way for yet another discovery. The recovery from my surgery in October 2013 was fairly easy, so about a week later, I checked on *23andMe* in case some new cousins showed up. I already knew from Mary Lou's results that we, as first cousins, shared about eleven percent of our chromosomes.

Of course, David was sharing my office space, and nearly fell off his chair when I said, "Oh, my God! You are not going to believe this."

As always, he panicked and thought there was something wrong with me, saying, "Are you OK?"

"Yes, yes, I'm fine, but there's someone in the relative list named Jacob Tanaka. We share about twelve percent of our chromosomes. The part I don't understand is *23andMe* shows him as my first cousin."

David scratched his head, "Well, although that sounds strange, I guess it's not impossible."

My mom had two brothers, and I knew their children. Both of them are older than I am. My dad had a lot of brothers and sisters, but I didn't know any of them. A lot of strange scenarios began running through my head, like one of my mother's brothers having a child out of wedlock that no one knew anything about. It was more likely that one of my dad's siblings had a child named Jacob, but I had never found him in tracing their families through genealogy.

I knew that the only way to understand this was to contact Jacob. I messaged him through 23andMe with a sharing request and got a quick response. We shifted to email communication, and I quickly learned that Jacob was twenty-eight years old, and he and his dad live in Hawaii. This made things even more confusing. How could my aunts and uncles have had a child so young? This would have meant that they were in their fifties or older when that child was born. Not impossible, but highly unlikely. Then there was the Japanese surname. Where did *that* come from?

David and I went crazy for weeks trying to figure out how I could possibly have a cousin who was only twenty-eight years old and had a Japanese last name. One thing I was sure of was that the relationship was on my father's side. Of course. Jacob had zero matches with Mary Lou, so it couldn't have been a love child from my mother's brothers. That was a relief. Once again, it presented me with yet another Latham mystery.

We sat for hours, with David saying, "Based on your parents' ages, and Mary Lou's age, we know that any first cousins would have to be much older."

"I know. And how on earth did I get Japanese people in my family? I know I don't have Japanese ancestry from *23andMe*, so it has to be through marriage."

We wracked our brains for an answer, doing repeated searching on the internet, and finally found that a shared percentage of that magnitude could also be from a nephew or niece. It might have been nice if *23andMe* had given us a hint that a match that high could also be a nephew. Now it made sense.

Jacob and I began to correspond regularly, and it turns out that he decided to do the *23andMe* testing for his father, Rodney, who had been adopted, and knew nothing about his birth parents. Many states seal adoption records, and to get them unsealed, you have to get a court order. Hawaii is one of those states. Rodney had never pursued that, and as far as I know, has still not. I think Jacob was more interested in understanding family history than his dad.

Rodney's adoptive father was Japanese, so Rodney had taken his name, Tanaka. Now we had two men with German first names and a Japanese last name. Hmmm. The bottom line was that I didn't find a cousin on *23andMe*. I found a nephew. This, of course, meant that his father was yet another half-brother, bringing us to six Latham children—that we know of so far.

After many discussions, David and I finally began to understand all of this. My nephew, Jacob, has twenty-two percent Japanese ancestry, so that means that his father, Rodney, would have about fifty percent. Jacob's mother was Caucasian, with German ancestry. Thus, his name.

The rest of Jacob's ancestry is Northern European. Much of it English, just like mine. Unlike Jacob, with about seventy-seven percent Northern European, my Northern European is ninety-nine percent, since I have no Japanese and only a smidgeon of Sub-Saharan African. My nephew and new half-brother knew from Rodney's adoptive parents that his birth mother was Japanese. Jacob's DNA testing showed us that Rodney's father must have been Clarence. After checking Clarence's service records for the appropriate time period, I confirmed he was indeed in Hawaii when Rodney would have been conceived. Bingo.

In his profile on *23andMe*, Jacob wrote, "I know nothing about my family history, that's the main reason I sent in my sample. So, I'm hoping to find relatives."

Like me, in beginning my discoveries with the *Genographic* results, Jacob had no idea what he'd uncover. Suddenly, Rodney went from being an only child to one of six. In addition, Jacob gained lots of aunts and uncles and cousins. I love corresponding with him. He calls me "Auntie."

My discovery of Jacob and Rodney led me back to trying to document our dad and the women he met along the way to produce the wonderful people we all are.

Part Three

The Mommas and the Poppa

"Parents rarely let go of their children, so children let go of them. They move on. They move away. The moments that used to define them—a mother's approval, a father's nod—are covered by moments of their own accomplishments. It is not until much later, as the skin sags and the heart weakens, that children understand; their stories, and all their accomplishments, sit atop the stories of their mothers and fathers, stones upon stones, beneath the waters of their lives."
MITCH ALBOM

Prologue

This part of *Sibling Revelries* contains the stories of our mothers and the common father my half-siblings and I share—to the extent that my brothers and sisters and I know them. There is a lot that we simply do not know. The narratives of the parents and the descriptions of their relationships are based on historical facts and what few shared sibling memories we have. Many of the facts were uncovered in genealogical searches, some from US Navy service records.

One mother's story is fictionalized to protect the requested privacy of her child and her family, who apparently knew little of her narrative. Another story—Yoshiko's—is completely invented, since we know nothing about her, other than she was pure-blooded Japanese. Some of the details, and any dialog in these chapters, are fictional and not based on any known facts, merely informed speculation and literary license.

Chapter Seventeen

Clarence, The Common Denominator

"Twenty years from now, you will be more disappointed by the things you didn't do than those you did. So throw off the bowlines. Sail away from safe harbor. Catch the wind in your sails. Explore. Dream. Discover."
MARK TWAIN

Clarence. Personal photo.

Clarence was born in July 1919, the youngest of ten children, to Thomas and Dora Latham. His oldest sibling, Ruth, was twenty when he was born, and the child ahead of him was fifteen months old. Two of the children died in infancy, so he grew up as one of eight, four girls and four boys.

Because he was the baby, he was as spoiled as a child could be in a household without great financial means.

Both his father, and especially his mother, doted on him, giving him whatever special treats they could afford. One of those was time with his father and older brothers.

Clarence's father and brothers loved to fish, and when they thought he was old enough to toddle down to the water and handle a rod and reel, they took him along. They gathered up their equipment, went out into their backyard, and dug up some fat, juicy night crawlers to entice the fish to bite on their hooks. Like most little boys, Clarence loved playing in the dirt, so he decided immediately that this fishing thing he'd been hearing about might be pretty keen.

He asked his Dad, "Do fish really like to eat these worms? They're fun to dig up, but they don't look good to eat to me."

Thomas just smiled, saying, "Fish like different things than we do, son. You like macaroni and cheese, right? Well, a fish wouldn't be at all interested in that."

At that point, Clarence learned a life lesson and decided he'd never try to eat worms.

Armed with lots of good bait, they set off from home, crossed the road, and walked down the little hill that was covered in wildflowers in the spring, to where the Salt River burbled along its way to empty into the Ohio River. Once they got to their favorite spot, near some rocks to stand on, and some gentle rapids, they began to school Clarence in the mysteries of fishing. He learned that hooks are not something you play with, especially after he saw those barbs on the ends. Then he watched as the worms were put on the hooks. He immediately understood that if they squirmed that much when they were threaded on, it would hurt like the dickens if he got one in his finger. He learned quickly to be very careful.

His next lesson was casting, and that one was a bit more difficult. Since he was still a little fellow, his lack of height worked against him. His brothers helped out with that by holding him up and guiding his arm. As time went on and he got taller, he knew exactly what to do, did it well, and was on his own. When he was still quite small, his brothers had to help him reel his fish in. That was OK with him. He'd rather have help than lose those fish. He learned to love his big brothers and fishing and it became a pastime that he enjoyed the rest of his life. He often brought in more fish than his brothers did. No one minded, since the fish they caught made a good dinner, and it was a nice change from the usual meals that Dora was able to scrape together with their limited means. This was back in the days when the Salt River was cleaner than it is now, and you could get catfish and even some small mouth bass occasionally. Both were tasty, and Dora knew just how to cook them.

Clarence lived in Shepherdsville until he was eleven, when his family moved to Louisville, where his dad found a better job. His early life from childhood until he entered high school was as pleasant as it could be in a family that wasn't wealthy. Clarence's outgoing personality allowed him to get along with most of the boys in his class, and his looks didn't hurt among the girls. Even the bullies didn't bother him. He was just too darned nice. In kindergarten, one kid, Sam, started to make fun of him for his name; the other kids ganged up on him. Sam never bothered him again. When other kids in his class had trouble with homework, he'd pitch in and help as much as he could. In addition, although he wasn't interested in team sports, he was always up for games on the playground like kick the can, tag, and marbles.

Beyond fishing, his true love, he also learned to bowl, and enjoyed that during his high school years. He was lucky, since Louisville had Vernon Lanes, a historic bowling alley that offered special pricing in the afternoons for school kids. The money he earned doing whatever errands he could find to do was enough to afford a couple of games. He went with his friends every time he could afford to and became a proficient bowler.

Clarence had a good home life. He had a large, close-knit family. Before moving to Louisville, they lived in a semi-rural area where he could easily fish and go exploring or hunting for squirrels any time he wanted to. In those days, it was safe for kids to go wandering by themselves or with their buddies, and he took advantage of that whenever he could. In summers, he was gone most days from sunup to sundown. Once he got to Louisville and into high school, his teenage hormones kicked in. Clarence discovered girls. He decided that he liked them—a lot. Even better than fishing or bowling.

Clarence realized that girls loved to dance, so he'd go to every dance he could for an excuse to get close to them without being slapped. His school had dances every Friday night. On one Friday, he went with some buddies and they scanned the crowd for pretty girls. Most of the girls were lined up on one wall, with the boys on the opposite one. One of the students played music that was gathered anywhere they could find it, sometimes from kids who came from wealthier families.

Clarence targeted one girl in particular, named Barbara. She was pretty, with long blond hair, cornflower blue eyes, and a perfect nose, thanks to the talents of Louisville's top plastic surgeon. When he got near her, he smelled orange and lavender, the main components of Elizabeth Arden's *Blue Grass* perfume. Clarence, of course, knew nothing about perfumes. He just knew she smelled good. Barbara was a cheerleader, so she was popular too, and one of the kids from a wealthier family. She acted and dressed like it, always in the latest fashions. He approached her and asked her to dance.

Barbara turned her surgically-perfect little nose up at him, saying, "I don't know you and I don't know your family, so you must be one of those poor kids from the other side of the tracks. I don't want to have anything to do with you."

He was mortified. However, being confident and not easily intimidated, he told her, "You may think you're pretty high and mighty and better than I am, but you don't know what you're missing." And he turned on his heel and walked away.

Although at this point in his life, he was attracted to blondes, he began to wonder if brunettes might be more level-headed and not so snotty. Clarence moved on and found a little brunette named Sally, who he thought was as cute as a bug's ear. He knew her from his math class. Sally was not high and mighty, so she agreed to dance with him.

Sally was angry at how Barbara had acted toward him and said, "I saw how that Barbara treated you. She thinks she's hot stuff, but she'll get hers someday."

Clarence not only thought Sally was a good dancer, but she also smelled good. Different than Barbara. Her fragrance wasn't perfumy. It was clean, kind of like Ivory soap. He soon realized she was also a nice person. During a slow dance, he especially enjoyed burying his face in her long, brunette hair and smelling her clean, fresh scent.

Sally wasn't the only one to experience Clarence's charm. Others enjoyed being near him too. A handsome boy, with dark blond wavy hair tending to curly, his piercing blue eyes reached into their souls. Clarence took his pleasant personality and learned in those years to morph it into charming when he was around girls. He could usually worm his way through their defenses. He stole many caresses and even the occasional kiss before being chased off. Unfortunately, like many teenage boys, he also discovered booze and tobacco.

Not everything in his life was idyllic, though. During his teen years in the 1930s, the United States was going through a crushing economic time that devastated many families. The Depression left every family who was not wealthy, and even some who were, with meager means at best, and they struggled as they never had before just to make ends meet. People had trouble finding and keeping jobs. Children had to drop out of school and lost both their childhoods and their educations to help their families survive. In many cases, those children were the sole providers, putting unbelievable pressure on them. Fortunately, Clarence's dad kept his job, and although his pay wasn't high, it was enough for them to get by on.

Unlike snotty Barbara's family, his family wasn't part of the "horsey set," the small group of people in Louisville who were heavily involved in the yearly Kentucky Derbies. In those circles, the women's biggest challenge was trying to decide what kind of hat to wear to the race. Clarence's mother's biggest challenge was trying to figure out how to feed her family. Dora faced that task every day, with eight children and a husband to feed and care for. She shopped for the lowest cost meat she could and dressed it up with local vegetables she bought from nearby farmers to make it more inviting. Those farmers were suffering too, and Dora and others like her, were some of their regular customers. Many nights, they had meatless meals, like Navy beans with lots of spices and maybe a ham bone if Dora could find one, or red beans and rice, but without the sausage that we're used to having in it.

Clarence's dad, Thomas, was a packer in a machine shop, putting the parts they made into containers for shipping. Most men at that time didn't have educations beyond high school, if they even had that. Clarence's dad had an eighth-grade education. His mother was a housewife. At that time, that wasn't unusual. Most women in those days were homemakers. They didn't work outside the home as many women do today. They furnished and decorated their homes as best they could, and they kept them clean. Doing laundry, washing dishes, and patching clothing that was starting to show signs of wear were constant chores. Darning socks, sewing clothing, and maybe knitting or crocheting—if they could get their hands on some inexpensive yarn—kept them occupied at night. On top of that, there was the never-ending grocery shopping and cooking. That represented their careers and left them little free time for themselves.

Clarence was handsome and intelligent; more quick-witted than well educated. He wasn't the least bit interested in school. It bored him, so he didn't try very hard. His grades reflected it, with high Cs and low Bs. Kids in those days weren't told that they had to go to college as they are now, unless they were from wealthy families. Clarence's family was far from wealthy, so that wasn't an option for him. Boredom soon got the better of him, and he dropped out of school after the eleventh grade. The only thing he missed were those dances where he could get close to the girls.

After he dropped out, he vowed he would never set foot in another school for the rest of his life. To help his family, and because anything was better than school, he got a job as a sales clerk at Bradbury's Pharmacy in Louisville, where he earned $18 a week. Not a fortune, but it certainly helped his family out.

Clarence was pleased to have a pretty easy job, not dirty and back breaking like factory work. On his first day, he asked a lot of questions, and proved to Mr. Bradbury that he was smart and willing to learn. In addition, he worked hard. Bradbury was pleased that he'd found a good worker.

At this well-known Louisville pharmacy, his duties were to sell patent medicines, drug sundries (miscellaneous things like bandages, antiseptics, petroleum jelly, etc.), make up the counter displays, and work behind the fountain, serving fountain drinks. Those were the days when any decent pharmacy had a soda fountain and served up milk shakes, ice cream sodas, and carbonated drinks. All of them appealed to the girls, which made this part of Clarence's job the most fun. Sally and many of his other friends came in so he was able to flirt and hear the latest school gossip. Even snotty Barbara would occasionally come in and would at least talk to him—if she wanted an ice cream soda, that was.

Clarence loved working at the fountain, but thought the patent medicines and drug sundries were a nuisance, since he had to replenish the shelves constantly, taking him away from the girls. He knew he didn't want to work in a pharmacy for the rest of his life. Being young and inexperienced, he wasn't sure just what he wanted to do.

Louisville in the 1930s was a story of significant economic extremes. From a hard to imagine unemployment rate of almost fifty percent in the early years of the decade, to a boom that began in 1937, it was a city of huge economic swings that most of the country never experienced. Due in large part to the repeal of Prohibition in

An example of a drug store soda fountain. Ames Tribune photo. Permission to reproduce courtesy of Ames Historical Society, © Ames Tribune. All Rights Reserved.

December 1933, and the newly built Seagram distillery, employment was up, and things were looking good. Many of the jobs at the distillery were filled by women who operated the bottling line. For Clarence, the prospect of working in a liquor factory didn't sound appealing, even if it paid more than Bradbury's Pharmacy, and might put him in close contact with some cute girls. He preferred drinking it—preferably good Kentucky bourbon—to making and bottling it.

January 1937 brought something else besides economic prosperity to Louisville, a flood of immense proportions. In that one event, the area received half the rain it would get for the entire year. Clarence's family lived in on Mellwood Drive, just outside Louisville. Their home fronted Beargrass Creek, a tributary of the Ohio River. When the Ohio flooded, so did Beargrass Creek, and so did Clarence's home. Three feet of water and mud rushed in and covered everything in their house. They had to split up and live with relatives for months while they shoveled and swept Beargrass Creek out of their rooms.

Once they did, they had to fight the mold and mildew that follow every flood before they could move back in. In addition to the emotional toll it exacted, it was miserable, backbreaking, smelly work. Just the kind of thing Clarence hated.

Clarence had to pitch in and help. Seeing his family's suffering, he realized there had to be something, somewhere, that was better than Kentucky. He knew that he didn't want to stay in Louisville and knew for certain that he didn't intend to end up like his brothers and sisters. They were busy living life one day to the next, with no adventure or excitement.

Bored beyond belief, Clarence wanted thrills in his life. In 1938, songs like "I've Got a Pocketful of Dreams" and "Nice Work If You Can Get It" were playing on the radio. There was no TV yet, so with an active imagination, he could visualize the stories that those songs portrayed. Clarence could see exactly how those songs played out in his head.

Films like *You Can't Take It with You* and *The Adventures of Robin Hood* were playing at movie theaters. Both of these films were playing at the end of the Great Depression, when people's spirits were sorely in need of a boost. *You Can't Take It with You* was a zany comedy about a man from a wealthy family who becomes engaged to a woman from a hilariously eccentric, non-conformist family. It was pure escapism. *The Adventures of Robin Hood* played directly to Clarence's desire for adventure. If Robin Hood could steal from the rich and give to the poor, maybe he could do something exciting with his life. All this popular culture heavily influenced Clarence's thoughts and dreams. Since he never finished high school, his chances of landing a really good job were slim to none (*Nice Work*

If You Can Get It). But he certainly had his pockets full of dreams, and he knew they wouldn't be realized in Louisville. He wanted laughs like they had in *You Can't Take It with You*, and adventure, like Robin Hood. To this now eighteen-year old, excitement was *always* a good thing.

Before and during World War I, Navy recruiting posters said "Join the Navy and See the World!" In the late 1930s they were all about pride, tradition, and fighting. There was one in particular that caught Clarence's eye. It featured a sexy girl saying *"Gee!! I wish I were a man. I'd join the Navy. Be a Man and Do It."* What red-blooded, high-spirited eighteen-year old could resist those appeals? In 1938, he enlisted.

US Navy Recruiting Poster. Image by Howard Chandler Christy. Originally developed during World War I. Public domain image.

During these turbulent times, some boys became men. Other boys became men physically, but still thought and acted like undisciplined teenagers. Clarence was one of them. Girls grew up too quickly, becoming wise beyond their years and yearning for more than just a day-to-day existence. And they loved men in uniforms. That was a further incentive for Clarence to join up.

During the late 1930s, Hitler was making his presence known in Europe, but that was not uppermost in most Americans' consciousness. They were preoccupied trying to make ends meet. Hitler was not perceived then as the evil monster he soon showed the world he was, unless you were from Austria or Czechoslovakia. In fact, Time magazine named him "Man of the Year" in 1938, and an English magazine did a profile puff piece on his country chalet in the Bavarian Alps, near the Austrian border. He was just an interesting person. Unless you lived in Europe and were Jewish.

Even fewer Americans knew anything about what the Japanese might be up to. At that time, they weren't thinking about the Americans. They were busy invading nearby China.

Clarence didn't know much about the Navy, but he figured anything had to be better than staying in Louisville. He didn't like the idea of the Army, where he'd have to do forced marches with heavy backpacks. Too much physical labor. His starting pay was a whopping $21 a month. While this was about half the minimum wage at the time, and significantly less than his pay at Bradbury's, it was a start, and a way out of Louisville. Most importantly, it gave him a chance at that adventure and excitement he longed for so much. Those motivators always have a price, and Clarence would soon learn their price could be more than just financial.

The beginning of his Navy adventure was the Great Lakes Naval Training Station near Chicago, Illinois. Although it was still the Midwest, it was a big city, and was much more exciting than dull old Louisville with its smelly distillery. Clarence arrived on Navy transportation with a busload of other young recruits. When they rode through the massive gates and past the guard shack, he knew this was something the likes of which he'd never seen. Of course, Chicago itself was big, but the base was enormous—much larger than he'd expected. It was like a city within a city. There were barracks, parade grounds, and row after row of buildings dedicated to training. On top of that, there were people coming and going everywhere.

US Naval Training Center, Great Lakes. Clarence's first stop. From a postcard produced in the 1930s. Permission to reproduce from CardCow.com.

He arrived in November to a cold, biting wind blowing off Lake Michigan. Coming from moderate, warm Louisville, this was a shock to his system. He reminded himself that this was the start of his great adventure, so he toughed it out. And, besides that, The Navy issued him a nice, toasty overcoat. But it did get to his ears. Although he was there only three months, that wind never let up, and his ears never got warm. In addition, there was a period of five days where the high temperature never got above freezing. It certainly wasn't Louisville. And that was more good than bad.

He met many fellow recruits from all over the country during the time he was there. Some of them were even in his same classes. One of them was George, a lanky farm boy from Tennessee. George liked to drink as much as Clarence did, so they bonded pretty quickly. They discovered bars when they could get off base—which wasn't often enough for them. On one occasion, George managed to smuggle in some whiskey and he and Clarence drank it up before their superiors could find it. Then they were caught. They were split up into separate barracks, and George was transferred into another class. That was the end of those adventures. They were both assigned to mess duties, peeling potatoes and washing dishes for a month. Much to Clarence's dismay, he never found another co-conspirator again.

Although it was exciting and adventurous, at the NTS Clarence learned the Navy meant business, and he had to be *where* they wanted him to be *when* they wanted him to be there. This irritating requirement didn't mix well with his plans. He ended up being absent over leave (AOL, as the Navy calls it), on several occasions. He paid the price for those youthful indiscretions by losing his shore leave. That shore leave was one of his main priorities, and the loss of it stung. On another occasion, he was AOL and found drunk and disorderly in a bar with some of his buddies. George wasn't the only one he drank with. The MPs hauled him in. That experience resulted in the loss of eighteen dollars of his twenty-one dollars monthly pay for two months. This was a very expensive lesson; unfortunately, Clarence didn't learn from it.

His next stop was the USS Oklahoma, based at the time in San Diego, California, far from Louisville and cold, windy Chicago, and not just geographically. When he arrived, he was once again amazed at the size of the base. At nearly 1,000 acres, it contained a training station, a hospital, an airfield, a submarine base, and dock after dock for ships.

He learned quickly that San Diego had a great climate and the base provided a constant buzz of excitement with Sailors and Marines everywhere. Plus, of course, it had pretty California girls. There were opportunities to have shore leave to explore this intriguing and beguiling place, with its always-pleasant weather, palm trees, beaches, and beautiful people. San Diego was not far from Los Angeles, where there were movie stars and hordes of good-looking girls who hoped to be movie stars. He went there as often as he could.

So, what did the Navy do to this boy who hated school? They put him into school! Clarence didn't realize the Navy needed people with specific skills, and they got them by training their new recruits. The Navy decided his niche was as a Corpsman. Navy Corpsmen provide treatment for Sailors or Marines, doing whatever it takes to keep them fit and ready to serve. Their duties at that time were varied, and included assistance to physicians and dentists with surgeries, specialization in radiology, search and rescue, optical, or preventive medicine. They often transported the sick and injured to safe quarters. They were interesting jobs, and Clarence certainly had the ability to handle his duties, as long as he was motivated.

His initial Corpsman training began with the pedagogical portion. Classes were held all day, and the trainees didn't get to have liberty often. In spite of this rigor, he told himself it was better than a liquor factory, the training was only 9 weeks, and you couldn't beat San Diego. He finished smack in the middle of his class and ended up with a grade of eighty-two. Not bad for someone who hated formal education. One of his best grades was for Hygiene & Sanitation; his worst was in Chemistry. I find it ironic that he bore a daughter who earned a Bachelor's degree in Chemistry. So, Clarence was clean, but he couldn't mix things well (except maybe drinks). He also did well in anatomy and physiology, perhaps from all the practice he'd gotten with the many girls he wooed.

From the end of his initial training, he was taught the military use of rifles and pistols, but he never did especially well in either. Strange for a country boy who spent a lot of his youth in the woods, shooting squirrels. He finally found his niche as a gun pointer, where he achieved first class rating.

During the next couple of years, he had five separate disciplinary actions, from AOLs to having clothing that belonged to another person—in this case, a woman—to violating parole. He lost money and he lost shore leave. He was miserable.

Perhaps living through these punishments woke him up, because after this, he had only a couple more infractions. And, in September 1940, he re-enlisted. He was immediately transferred to Portsmouth, New Hampshire, where he completed his Corpsman training. For the next twelve months, he studied and learned the details of being a Pharmacy and Dental Mate. His grades were good, and during that year, he engaged in no more activities requiring punitive actions. Maybe he was starting to grow up. By this time, he was twenty-two years old.

Clarence learned a lot in those early Navy days, but no one ever told him that it might be dangerous to associate with women who could procreate.

During his time in San Diego, he met the first of them. One in a string of The Silent Mothers—Ethel.

Chapter Eighteen

Ethel, "The First" of The Silent Mothers

"The sins of the Midwest: flatness, emptiness, a necessary acceptance of the familiar. Where is the romance in being buried alive? In growing old?"
STEWART O'NAN

Ethel. Personal photo.

Ethel was born in October, 1922 in Lawrence, Kansas. She was the oldest of five children, four girls, and one boy. Two of the girls died in early childhood, one at one-day old, the other two weeks before her first birthday, so that boy had to contend with only two girls growing up.

Ethel's parents were bona fide Midwesterners—her mother, Pauline, was born in Kansas. Her father, Charles Edward, who everyone called Eddie, came to this world in Nebraska. Before that, her grandparents and great-grandparents were from Indiana and Ohio. The Language Section Editor for the Humanities Institute at Ohio State University describes people from that part of the country as "strong, brave, polite, hard-working, self-effacing, self-sufficient, generous, friendly, Protestant, white, normal, average, and boring." Although she loved them dearly, as she grew up and became more adventurous, Ethel found them—and especially the places they lived—more boring than she imagined anyone and any place could possibly be.

Ethel's first American ancestors were more adventurous than those Midwesterners. On her father's side, several of them came into Virginia from Ireland in the early 1700s. On her mother's side, they emigrated from Scotland, and there were Revolutionary War Patriots on both sides. At that time, there was religious persecution in the British Isles as well as that experienced by my husband, David's, ancestors in Germany. England, Wales, Scotland, and Ireland were originally part of the Holy Roman Empire, and thus, the Catholic church. Only later did the Anglicans and other Protestant sects develop. Many Scots were victimized by James II for being practicing Presbyterians. Originally, they migrated to Northern Ireland, and some eventually made their way to America. Many of them came over as indentured servants to wealthy landowners or merchants. A step above slaves, if they were bought by the right people, they eventually earned their freedom, and possibly some land to start a new life in a new country.

Cross-Atlantic trips in those days were not what they are today, and if they had to come over in steerage, as most indentured servants did, it was pure hell. Like many other early American colonists, Ethel's ancestors migrated from Virginia and North Carolina, and then through the western frontier of Kentucky, finally finding their promised land in places like Illinois, Indiana, and Ohio. Her family eventually came to rest in Kansas. Ethel inherited a host of characteristics from all of them, including strong convictions, stubbornness, Scottish thriftiness, and an Irish temper.

During the 1920s and 1930s, Kansas was an even worse place to be than Louisville if you were young and looking forward to a better life. That better life meant not having to scrape and scrabble to stay alive from one day to the next. Like many other states, Kansas suffered deeply during the Great Depression, losing over 100,000 of its residents who fled to pursue a better life elsewhere. For those who stayed, drinking wasn't a possible diversion either. It was a "dry" state even before Prohibition, although people found ways to get around that. There were thriving speakeasies, and bootleggers who supplied illegal hooch to those who wanted it. Even with that availability, Ethel's family never indulged. It wasn't that they were teetotalers, they just didn't like it. And, they couldn't understand why anyone would enjoy it.

All of her more recent ancestors had been farmers or worked in an area related to agriculture their entire lives. After Ethel was born, her parents left Kansas to try to improve their lives. They went to Iowa, where Ethel's dad had a promising job offer.

Pauline encouraged and supported Eddie, "I certainly hope Iowa is better than Kansas. I see nothing here for us but one misery after another."

Eddie agreed, "You sure are right about that. With a bit of luck, we'll have more opportunities."

Like Clarence and his feelings about Kentucky, Ethel's parents knew they didn't want to live the rest of their lives in Kansas. Or Iowa, either, once they got there. They saw how their parents and their grandparents had lived and they understood how hard it was to try to make a decent living in the farm belt. They were ahead of their time in understanding that the traditional family farm would eventually become financially impractical.

Unfortunately, the Johnsons quickly discovered that things in Iowa in the 1930s were no better than they were in Kansas. Along with other goods, the prices of all farm products fell, and this had a devastating impact on those who worked the land or worked for them. There were repeated instances of strikes, driven by the farmers' demands that they receive payments for their products that were above their cost of production. In some places, dairy producers blocked the roads to stop delivery of milk and cream to market. If the driver didn't turn back, the strikers would dump the milk rather than receive pay ments below their costs. Ethel's parents saw this and it upset one of their strong convictions. You never wasted food, no matter what. They certainly understood the farmers' frustration, but it intensified their desire to get out and away from farming communities.

A milk blockade in Iowa. Permission to reproduce from the State Historical Society of Iowa, Des Moines.

To compound their misery, the entire mid-section of the country was suffering from the Dust Bowl. As the farmers' fates went, so did the surrounding communities. And, so did the fate of Ethel's family. Ethel's dad lost his job. After doing everything they possibly could to survive, and like so many other Midwesterners, they decided to head west to California where there were more opportunities and jobs. The Johnsons left for Los Angeles in 1939. Ethel was seventeen. She was excited beyond belief, and couldn't wait to see more of the country, especially the ocean. The only bodies of water she'd ever seen were ponds.

They couldn't afford to travel by train, and only the wealthy traveled by airplane in those days, so they packed up two adults, three kids, and all of their possessions in their old Ford and drove. This wasn't like traveling as we're accustomed to now, in big SUVs or travel trailers. They were also the days before the Interstate Highway system, which didn't exist until the mid to late 1950s. Many of the roads that the Johnsons traveled in 1939 were marginal at best, not paved, and filled with hazards. Most of us would never think of trying to navigate them unless we had a 4-wheel drive vehicle. Nevertheless, many thousands of Americans did it. They had no other choice. It was that or stay put and stay hungry. And that was not a good option.

Much of the Johnsons' trip was on the legendary Route 66, which runs from Chicago through Missouri, Kansas, Oklahoma, Texas, New Mexico, and Arizona before ending in Los Angeles. Hailed as the "Main Street of America," Route 66 stretched nearly 2,500 miles, and became the means to an end in the search for a better life for hundreds of thousands of people. They were mostly white, and they were mostly poor. This kind of travel wasn't easy going in the 1930s. The original Route 66 was primarily gravel and graded dirt. Fortunately, Ethel's parents' timing was good—the entire stretch was paved in 1938.

Lange, Dorothea, photographer. Family of nine from Fort Smith, Arkansas, trying to repair their car on road between Phoenix and Yuma, Arizona. On their way to try to find work in the California harvests. May, 1937. Image retrieved from the Library of Congress, https://www.loc.gov/item/fsa2000001087/PP/. (Accessed February 15, 2017.) Library of Congress, Prints & Photographs Division, FSA/OWI Collection, LC-DIG- LC-DIG-fsa-8b31910.

For Pauline and Eddie, the trip was an exercise in keeping the car running, the kids' stomachs full, and just staying alive from one day to the next. To Ethel, who had spent her entire childhood in Iowa, and was more than ready to get away from those endless boring years, it was a monumental adventure. They picked up Route 66 in St. Louis, a big, bustling city with tall buildings the likes of which Ethel had never seen. They passed through Tulsa and Oklahoma City and north Texas, eventually getting to Amarillo, home of the Amarillo Livestock Auction. Ethel had seen cows before, but the cows she knew were dairy cows. Those Amarillo "cows" were real cattle, and the cowboys who were wrangling them were real cowboys, not dairy farmers. It was just like it looked in the movies. Ethel swooned over them and thought they were killer dillers. Her parents stayed busy trying to keep her away from them.

Santa Fe and Albuquerque brought her a glimpse of how different life was for American Indians and Mestizos. She made friends with an Apache girl and absorbed the culture like a piece of fry bread soaking up the juice from a bowl of soup. Ethel learned that there were more uses for corn and beans than she ever thought possible, and how mild and hot chilies could be used to flavor soups and stews. This was a far cry from the meat and potatoes she was used to, and she loved it. The journey was truly an adventure for her. She saw more of the country than she ever dreamed she would and gained an appreciation for cultures outside the farm belt. It was a huge revelation for a Midwestern girl.

From New Mexico, they pressed on to Tucson, Arizona, where her dad worked for a short time for Warner Brothers Studio. In 1940, they were making a Western called *Arizona*, starring William Holden and Jean Arthur, and it was filmed on the Double U Guest Ranch. Ethel's Dad even had his picture taken with the then-famous actor. She became totally star struck and couldn't wait to get to California where she just knew that there would be more gorgeous men.

Later that year, they made it to Los Angeles, which Ethel decided was the closest thing to heaven she'd ever seen. The climate was great, and it was a big, thriving city. It was even bigger than St. Louis, and more exciting, especially with those movie stars that she'd see from time to time. She finished high school and got a good job with the telephone company. Ethel developed friendships with many of the other women who worked there, and quickly became captivated with the young sailors and Marines that came up from San Diego, flooding LA with handsome men in uniforms.

They became enchanted with her in turn. She had beautiful, wavy, brunette hair, sparkling hazel eyes that held a hint of mischief, and a great personality, although she was a bit shy when she first met someone. She dated and danced her way through boatloads of those swabbies and platoons of jarheads. Her best friend, Nancy, who worked with her at the telephone company, saw her the next morning after a night of dancing. Nancy had grown up in LA, so the guys in uniform weren't the novelty they were to Ethel.

She grinned and asked Ethel, "Say, who was that swell-looking guy I saw you with last night? You two were doing some serious dancing. And, you were awfully close during those slow dances."

Ethel blushed, "His name is Clarence, and he's from Kentucky. He's very charming, has a little bit of a Southern accent, which I think is cute, and is a smooth dancer. I think he really likes me."

Nancy warned her, "Better watch out for those sailors, Ethel, I've heard they can talk you into things you might not want to do."

Ethel was having the time of her young life, so she shrugged this off, "I know how to be careful, and besides, I just met him."

Clarence had begun to look more like a man and less like a boy by 1940 and could really charm the socks off the girls. By this time, he'd had a lot of practice with his many shore leaves and encounters with pretty girls who quickly became captivated with him. He knew exactly how to flatter them, telling them how beautiful and interesting they were. That charm also showed in the way he got them to tell him about themselves. Clarence was a good listener and could use the insights he gained by that probing to influence those girls to his way of thinking—which was to ultimately get them into bed.

He was immediately attracted to Ethel and wooed her every time he could get up to LA, taking her to dinner, dancing, and the movies. Dinner and movies were good, but just as in his high school days, what he really enjoyed was dancing. They went to USO parties, and Clarence got her to slow dance with him every chance he got. He enjoyed feeling the luscious curves of a girl's body next to his. Ethel didn't stand a chance. She was only eighteen and had never had any man as interested in her as Clarence was, and she loved to hear his stories too. Besides, being held so close by a handsome man was pretty exciting.

She eventually gave in completely to his charms and found herself doing a lot more than dancing and dining. All that closeness while dancing led to the bedroom of the hotel where he was staying. Although Ethel was very nervous about this, Clarence put some music on the radio and got her dancing and swaying with him. One thing led to another, and Clarence achieved his goal of getting Ethel into bed.

A couple months later, she discovered she was pregnant. Her parents were horrified, and so was she. To make them feel better, she assured them that Clarence was a really nice guy, and he wanted to get married and have more kids.

Although the practical side of her knew she could make it work, Ethel was not totally thrilled about it either. This meant the end of her fun and forced her to grow up fast. Her family knew in their hearts that "nice" Midwestern girls didn't do things like that, and they raised their Ethel to be a nice girl. if they did, and were caught, the offending male did the right thing and made the girl an honest woman. Most importantly, no one *ever* talked about it. It was a family disgrace. At least they hoped and prayed that this charming man would make an honest woman of their little girl. He eventually did, but he didn't do it quickly enough to suit them.

Clarence was transferred to the huge Naval Base in Norfolk, Virginia, in February 1941. Navy life is not known for its stability, and since they had no idea where he might be stationed next and when, Ethel moved in with his parents in Louisville. Dora, poor Clarence's mother, had yet another mouth to feed, and it was one that was eating for two.

Ethel and Clarence were finally married in North Carolina in April of that year. Ethel was pleased, thinking *it's about time.*

At the time of their marriage, Ethel was eighteen and five months pregnant. Clarence was twenty-one. In many ways, they were still just kids. During their wedding ceremony, and unbeknownst to Ethel, Clarence was supposed to be on duty in Norfolk. Of course, this meant he was AOL once again. He lost four shore liberties, leaving Ethel without a honeymoon, or even a husband, as a very young, very pregnant, very newly married bride. Worse, it was in Norfolk, where Ethel knew no one.

She didn't realize it then, but this was just the beginning of a behavioral trend, where Clarence promised to be with her. Sadly, he always found some reason not to be. He was starting to feel the pressure of not being his own man. Shortly after they were married, in addition to not being there for her, and his occasional slips that resulted in loss of shore leave, Clarence developed a medical problem. It wasn't anything serious, just a deviated septum in his nose, but the Navy wanted it fixed. He was shipped off to a naval hospital, where he had some minor surgery to repair it. Ethel was alone once again.

While she was pregnant, and Clarence wasn't there with her, Ethel wondered whatever happened to the contented married existence that she'd dreamed of, with that man who was so charming when he was romancing her. Still, when Clarence was home with her, he was as attentive and charismatic as ever, so Ethel thought she could lead him onto the straight and narrow, and things would get better. Women have always thought they can change their men. History and bitter experience tells them that they never can. Still, Ethel was young, naïve, and trying hard to be optimistic. She didn't know at the time that she was waging a war that could not be won.

In August 1941, while they were in Norfolk, Clarence and Ethel had a beautiful baby girl they named Carolyn. She was a happy baby, but grew into a sad little girl who never saw much of her father as she was growing up. Carolyn cried a lot and couldn't understand where her daddy was. Very few pictures of her when she was young showed even a hint of a smile. When asked, her mother told her curtly that he was off fighting the war and would never say any more. Ethel's anger at Clarence seemed to make Carolyn even sadder. She sensed something was wrong, but couldn't understand what it was, so her only outlet was to cry.

Shortly after Carolyn was born, Clarence was transferred to the Naval Base in Philadelphia, PA. Ethel was devastated. She had hoped Norfolk wouldn't last and that Clarence would be sent back to the West Coast. Instead, she got Philadelphia. By this time, she had become a California girl, and she didn't want to be away from there, where her parents could spend time with her and Carolyn.

While they were in Philadelphia, thanks to more of what Clarence considered excruciating Navy schooling, he was promoted to Pharmacist's Mate. The Navy probably figured all that experience at Bradbury's Pharmacy in Louisville could be leveraged. They finally transferred Clarence back to San Diego later in 1942. Ethel and Carolyn decided to live in LA, so they could be close to Ethel's parents. At least there, they'd have some stability, and Carolyn would have a family surrounding her as she was growing up.

Although Clarence was in the Navy, he was not in a dangerous situation. At least not at first. That would soon change. In December 1941, the Japanese attacked the US Naval base in Pearl Harbor, Hawaii. By then, Clarence was stationed there, on the USS Oklahoma, one of the ships that was hit brutally in the attack. She sank after being repeatedly bombed and taking five torpedo hits. The Oklahoma rolled over within twelve minutes after the first bombs began falling along battleship row, stopping only when her masts touched bottom and she capsized. In addition to the thirty-two men who were wounded, 429 sailors on the Oklahoma out of a crew of about 2,200 lost their lives that day. The United States finally entered the war.

However, Clarence was luckier than his lost shipmates. He was on shore when the Japanese attack came, loading

The USS Oklahoma capsized in the foreground, with the USS Maryland behind her. The USS West Virginia burns furiously on the right. Image by the United States Navy. Caption from the National Archives and Records Administration via Wikipedia. Public domain image.

up on pharmacy supplies for the ship. Many of his buddies that he'd developed close relationships with were not so fortunate. These men were not just fellow sailors; they were his drinking pals and good friends. Clarence suffered the second major emotional jolt of his life. For days, he was numb, and in denial that this could have happened. In time, he finally came to grips with it, and he moved from denial to anger—at the Japanese and the war that caused this slaughter. His grief over the loss of his friends was intensified by feelings of guilt at not being with them. Clarence was in a deep depression for months afterwards, trying to understand why this had happened to them and not him. His way of dealing with it was to get a tattoo to honor his fallen comrades, and by drinking more heavily than ever. The memories of that day haunted him for the rest of his life and led to nightmares in which he'd wake up screaming at his friends to get out of the ship.

With the start of the war, Ethel was on the home front with a young baby. Along with the prospect of a long spell before Clarence might come home.

As she was growing up, Carolyn spent a lot of time with her mother's parents, especially her grandmother Pauline, whom Carolyn called Grammie P. They lived nearby, which made things easier for Ethel, and provided a sense of family and escape. Their house always smelled wonderful, since her Grammie P loved to bake. She made Carolyn treats like hot fudge pudding cake. Sugar cookies were one of their perennial favorites. As Carolyn grew older, her Grammie P taught her baking secrets. Soon, Carolyn became an accomplished baker. Ethel was pleased to have her show off her skills at home, and Carolyn would frequently take treats to her friends at school. They were always delighted to have lunch with her, since there were often goodies in her lunch box.

When Carolyn was young, Grammie P always read aloud to her, from *Winnie-the-Pooh*, and one of Carolyn's favorites, *Stuart Little*. As she got older, they read together, and compared notes on what they liked about the stories. They especially enjoyed the Nancy Drew mysteries and tried to outguess each other on who the bad guys were. They played games like checkers and Chutes and Ladders constantly. She loved her grandmother dearly and re-members the times she spent with her as the happiest of her childhood.

In July 1942, when Carolyn was only a year old, Clarence was assigned to one of the Naval Construction Battalions, The Seabees, and promptly left with them for the South Pacific. The Seabees were a new military group then. Nearly 200,000 men strong, they were master craftsmen who helped to ensure victory for the allies in the Pacific by building airfields in inhospitable environ-ments. They hacked through jungle growth and blasted coral so our troops could advance toward Tokyo. Clarence helped to care for these men as a Chief Pharmacist's mate. Like his shipmates, his service entitled him to wear a Bronze Star on his Asiatic-Pacific Campaign Ribbon. This was a big improvement over the AOLs of his earlier days.

Clarence served the Seabees in the Ellice Islands—now called Tuvalu. The Americans arrived in October 1942, and built a landing field at Funafuti atoll. That was the first step of many for the American forces in their northern drive toward the Gilbert Islands, which were occupied by the Japanese at the time.

In November 1943, Clarence re-enlisted for another four years. Ethel simply could not believe it. She was convinced that he'd quit and come home to her and Carolyn. This was Clarence's way of dealing with losing his buddies. He'd do anything he could to help kill those Japs who took his buddies from him. By this time, he had grown three inches, but would prove that he had still not grown up. In October 1944, he was transferred to San Diego, and given thirty days' leave. Ethel was ecstatic—she'd have him for a whole month. She thought she'd gotten her husband back, even if only for a short while.

Even when he was home with Ethel, he'd sneak out to bars. Ethel was furious and ended up searching the local haunts for him and dragging his inebriated butt home. No one in her family drank, so she was not used to this kind of behavior. Of course, her parents pointed out to her that this is what happens when you associate with a sailor. It infuriated her that Clarence would go out boozing rather than spending time with her and Carolyn. Many of those times, she'd find him with floozies who were as busy consuming his charm as they were swigging hooch. Ethel, with her stubborn streak in high gear, decided to give it another year.

Ethel finally began to realize that she'd made a lot of serious mistakes. It was bad enough that she got pregnant, but marrying this boozer was a bigger blunder. In June 1945, when Carolyn was four years old, she filed for divorce. She never wanted to think about or see Clarence again. Or talk about him with anyone, even his own child. She finally came to the conclusion that he was a total bastard, and by not talking about him she could rid her life, and her child's, of him forever.

Carolyn was a little over a year old while Clarence was in the South Pacific, and she had never known her father. She certainly knew nothing about what he was doing for the war effort. In fact, she was far too young to understand what war was. She knew that she had no daddy, and she didn't know why.

She grew up always wondering where her father was, and by the time she was three, he did something for which she'd never forgive him. She became very ill with a high fever and was put into isolation in the hospital. He never once came to see her. Of course, this was because he was off in the South Pacific serving his country. Ethel never told Carolyn that. Not then, and not ever. Carolyn only learned where he was at the time when I sent her his service records decades later.

While Carolyn was in the hospital, Los Angeles experienced some rare heavy rains that lasted for days, and when she hears heavy rain, even today, she thinks about that experience. She detests rain.

Carolyn was too young to understand the emotions and issues her mother was trying to deal with. As she got older, she probably would have understood. But Ethel kept her silence. It was her mistake, and a period of her life she simply didn't want to share.

Several years later, Ethel remarried. Willis was tall and scrawny, with thinning lank brown hair that he combed over, and boring brown eyes, not nearly as handsome or as charming as Clarence. His one redeeming quality was that he acted like a grown man. He was a good provider and treated Ethel much better than Clarence had. Most importantly, he didn't run around drinking and carrying on with other women.

Although he was a better fit for Ethel, he was far from that for Carolyn. This new husband didn't want to have someone else's child around. For her part, Carolyn couldn't stand being around someone who ignored her or talked down to her, so a lifelong mutual aversion developed. He was not the dad she had always wished for. Carolyn spent less and less time at home, and more and more time with her beloved grandmother. She still wanted to know more about her real father. Her mother wasn't having any part of that.

Chapter Nineteen

Maria, "The Woman with a Desire"

*"There are two tragedies in life. One is to lose
your heart's desire. The other is to gain it."*
GEORGE BERNARD SHAW

Maria. iStock photo.

Maria was born in Lynch, Kentucky in June 1915 to an
Italian immigrant father and a mother whose parents had
both emigrated from Ireland. This combination made her
a beauty. She had long, thick, wavy brunette hair and dark
brown eyes with flecks of gold that looked like the sun was
about to burst out of them. Her friends teased her about
how dark they were, calling her meatball eyes. Since she
also inherited a temper when the situation demanded it,
she pushed the ones she didn't like around, and laughed
over it with those she did.

Lynch is in Harlan County, in the southeastern part of Kentucky, just across the state line from West Virginia. At one time, it was the largest coal camp in the United States. It's in what's referred to as Appalachia, and images of poor children in dilapidated houses depict life for many in this part of the country. Like a lot of other towns where coal was discovered, Lynch was built by a coal company. In this case, it was the US Coal and Coke Company (now part of US Steel), and it was named for the head of the company, Thomas Lynch. It was a company town: the coal company owned the houses, the stores, and everything else. The citizens of Lynch had to pay the company for everything they needed to live. Tennessee Ernie Ford described it best in his popular song, *Sixteen Tons*. The coal was good there, there was a high demand for it, and there was a lot of it.

By the 1940s, Lynch had a population of more than 10,000 and even had its own hospital and movie theatre. Those were the glory days for Lynch. They weren't for Maria and her family.

Lynch was a big town even early in the new century when Maria was born, and her father, like most of the other men there who were immigrants with no education or training, worked in the mines, extracting the coal from the sedimentary seams of shale and sandstone.

During this time, John L. Lewis worked to actively organize the United Mine Workers and called for strikes to improve working conditions. Throughout the 1920s and well into the 1930s, the company, along with many other coal producers, did everything in their power to prevent unionization. The company had its own police force and used it brutally to keep union organizers out of the coal camp to intimidate miners who tried to join the union.

This action by the coal companies and the reactions of the miners led to confrontations and earned Harlan County the name of "Bloody Harlan." On many occasions, the miners laid in wait to ambush the company guards, paid thugs known as goons, on their patrols. The guards, for their part, went to miners' homes to flush out and rough up those they considered the union ringleaders. Miners were trampled with the guards' horses, and their heads were cracked open with Billy Clubs, leaving them bloody and unconscious, for their families to treat them. Those striking miners obviously couldn't use the company hospital in town.

Maria witnessed this violence first hand and swore no one would ever treat her that way and that she'd get out of Appalachia as soon as she could. It also hardened her. She decided she'd do whatever it took to get what she wanted. Maybe that ever-present coal dust darkened Maria's outlook as well as her surroundings, making her manipulative and egotistical.

Coal mining was dirty, backbreaking work, and was far more dangerous then than it is today. Although the mines were hazardous, Maria's father managed to avoid catastrophes on the job. But in his leisure time, he and her mother were in a terrible automobile accident. They were driving on an icy, hilly road one winter night, and her dad lost control of the car on a sharp curve. They ended up in a steep rocky ditch, with the front of the car landing driver's side down. There were no seat belts in cars then, and her dad was pinned between the door, the steering wheel, and the engine, suffering two broken legs and a crushed chest. He died immediately. Maria was twelve. She grieved deeply for her father for years.

Her mother survived and subsequently remarried, and Maria and her younger sister, Gina, became stepchildren.

Unlike Carolyn's experience, and the traditional wicked step-parent story, Maria loved her stepfather, John, dearly. In fact, she felt he treated her better than her biological father ever did. She thought he treated her and her sister even better than his own two biological children. Being a kind man, he did everything he could for those girls to make up for the loss of their father. He walked them to school, took them for ice cream once a month, and treated Maria and Gina like princesses on their birthdays. Her new father worked on the mechanical equipment at the mine, a much safer occupation than Maria's biological father's job, so she and her mother had fewer worries than they did when her biological dad was in the mines.

Like Maria, her mother and step-father also vowed to get out of the dependent company town that Lynch was in those days. When her step-father had a chance at a better job, Maria's new family moved to London, Kentucky. London was a real city—not anything like the coal mining town of Lynch, and it was much cleaner and prettier. Demographically, it was roughly ninety-five percent Caucasian, so Maria never had an opportunity to experience a wide range of ethnic diversity growing up. She and her family thought of non-Caucasians as "those people." Not only did they not socialize with them, but they certainly would never consider a long-term relationship with them or go so far as to bear children of mixed races.

When Maria was eighteen and Gina sixteen, they struck out on their own and moved to Lexington. London was nice, but it was no place for young women starting their lives. There just weren't as many opportunities there as there were in a bigger city. Lexington, with about twenty-five times the population of London, was in the heart of

Kentucky's Bluegrass Region, where jobs were available for smart young women. Plus, there were more opportunities to meet good looking young men. By 1936, Maria, now twenty-one, was working in the offices at the newly-formed Keeneland, now one of the premier horse breeding and racing facilities in the state. Gina was still finishing school. Best of all, they were not that far from their family's new home in London, so they were able to visit often.

Keeneland began operations with a race track and were the first in Kentucky to install a totalizator, a machine that automatically showed the total number and amounts bet on each horse. It works out the odds of the horse winning, and the payouts for what's called pari-mutuel betting, where the winnings are proportional to the bet made. In 1937 and 1938, they began showing geldings and auctioning thoroughbreds. Geldings are castrated stallions that may be problematic if they are easily distracted by other horses, difficult to handle, or otherwise not running to their full potential due to behavioral issues. Not all of them were problematic, and many made good mounts for those who just wanted a beautiful horse to ride. Thoroughbreds are pure-bred horses, usually with a long pedigree, known for their agility, speed and spirit. They are the race horses we think of and see in the Kentucky Derby and other prestigious horse races.

Besides racing, Keeneland was also notable for a lot of wealthy people. Maria and her sister became active in the horse-racing community, where they met a number of attractive young men. One of them was Adriano, a captivating Italian lad, with dark wavy hair, expressive deep brown eyes, and a winning smile. Not one of the wealthy people, Adriano was a first-generation American and he worked at Keeneland in a mechanical job. He was smitten with Maria. Adriano did everything he could to see her, thinking up any excuse to go to the office where Maria worked.

Finally, after summoning up his courage, he came in one day and asked her, "Would you like to go to a dance with me this evening?"

Maria was equally attracted to him, and knew she wouldn't take any guff from him, so she warned him, "Yes, as long as you act like a gentleman. Because if you don't, I will walk out on you and you'll never see me again."

"I promise you, I will be the best gentleman you can imagine. And we'll have fun!"

Adriano was indeed a gentleman, being raised by two parents who were born in Italy and valued family and good manners. His father immigrated to the United States early in the century, then returned to Italy and brought his wife and some cousins back with him several years later. The family travelled from Europe to America on the Mauritania, part of the Cunard Line.

Although this ship was a luxury liner, Adriano's father and mother came to America in steerage, so called because it was in the stern of the ship, near the steering gear. Ships at that time had three classes of passenger accommodation, First, Second, and Third, going from best to worst. Many immigrants who had virtually nothing, had to make do with accommodations below Third-Class quality, in steerage "quarters" designed for carrying large numbers of poor people as cheaply as possible. He shared his accommodations with 400 other people who slept in one compartment. The snoring made it nearly impossible to get any sleep. When that subsided, the babies would start crying, so there was virtually no rest. The food was poor, and the smells could be overwhelming, especially during rough weather when access to the upper deck was restricted.

Like his father before him, Adriano started working in the coal mines of southeastern Kentucky. Similar to Maria's step-father, and because he had an aptitude for any kind of mechanical apparatus, he worked on the equipment that was used in the mines, not in the blasting and digging and hauling. The fact that he was good at it, coupled with his experience in Lynch, provided him a wealth of knowledge. He could fix just about anything and keep it running in tip-top shape. Adriano was skilled in the use of various tools, could read blueprints and drawings, and was especially good at welding and troubleshooting. This allowed him to move to Lexington and get a job in a better environment. Unlike where he'd been, Lexington was a great place. It was a much bigger, more exciting city, and he loved being around the gorgeous horses and even more, the lovely Maria.

Adriano continued to be a gentleman, and he and Maria went to more and more dances. They did the Jive, the Jitterbug, the Lindy, and The Big Apple, laughing and getting breathless along the way. There were dance contests, and Adriano and Maria were good enough to win quite a few of them.

Maria took Adriano to London for some good home-made Italian food and to meet her parents. They tore into the antipasto, lasagna, chicken parmigiana, and tiramisu her mom had prepared, and soon were so stuffed they could barely move. Her family became very fond of him and appreciated how he treated their Maria.

They were married not long after this visit and started to enjoy their life. Their wedding was small, with Maria's and Adriano's family and some close friends in attendance. They took their vows at St. Paul Catholic Church and swore they would never be parted. There was a reception following the ceremony in the parish hall, with a variety of Italian foods cooked by the mothers, and Italian Cream wedding cake and coffee. Maria's sister, Gina, caught the bouquet.

Misfortune stepped in again, when her much-loved stepfather died of lung cancer, leaving her mother a widow again. He suffered for two years before the disease took him. Maria's mother, Maria, and Gina shared duties caring for him before he eventually had to be hospitalized, where he passed away peacefully. Her mother and her step-sister and step-brother came to live with Maria, Adriano, and Gina in Lexington, and her mother helped take care of the house and raising the step-children They all took an active role in raising those two. It wasn't an easy life, with money tight due to having to feed three more mouths, but it was a good one.

Everyone in this big family loved each other dearly, and enjoyed being part of the large equestrian community there. They were all good cooks and ate a lot of homemade pasta, paired with cheese and wine, and polished that off with heavy jolts of espresso. Plus, having those teenage stepchildren in the house kept it lively. Maria and her mother were always very close, and she had missed her when she was in Lexington and her mom was in London. She was thrilled to have her mother living with them, and it freed her up even further to pursue her career.

Although life was good, there was one thing that made it less than perfect. Maria's challenge was the climate in Lexington. Although it was a pretty place, it had hot, humid summers that wreaked havoc with her curly hair.

That was only a minor annoyance. It would start the day looking good, and then go totally haywire as soon as she stepped out the door. It constantly got in her face and even made her consider getting it cut short so it would be less of a problem to deal with.

Beyond having major hair issues, Maria quickly discovered that Lexington was called the allergy capital of North America at that time for good reason. She did fine in Lynch and London, but soon began to have horrible sensitivity, with a constantly stuffy, runny nose and watery, itchy eyes when she moved to Lexington. She had what people back then called "hay fever," and it made her miserable. That beautiful Kentucky bluegrass which covered Keeneland did not agree with her, and she sniffled and sneezed from springtime all the way through to the fall when the grass was pollinating.

Maria and Adriano loved children, wanted at least one of their own. Her mother said a prayer every night for grandchildren—soon.

She'd ask Maria, "So, when am I gonna have some beautiful little bambinos to cuddle and spoil?"

Despite their best efforts, Maria could not become pregnant. She told her mother that due to her allergies, she and Adriano decided to move to Hawaii.

They thought that perhaps a sunny, warm, climate without Kentucky bluegrass would be just the change they needed. Hawaii didn't have the tree or grass allergies that the mainland did, and they hoped that its beauty might help them work some reproductive magic. By then, her step-siblings had grown up and they were there for her mother in case she needed help. Although her mother didn't like losing her oldest daughter, moving became an easy choice for Maria and one from which her nose would derive great pleasure.

Maria and Adriano arrived in Hawaii in 1942, in Honolulu. They got off the plane to the most beautiful place they had ever seen. It didn't look real, with its lush palm trees and tropical flowers in profusion. Kentucky had certainly never looked like this. The air was sweet and warm, and there was no pollen to torture Maria's nose. There were gorgeous beaches that flanked an ocean that was an astounding cobalt blue color. They couldn't wait to dip their toes into it.

Both Maria and Adriano got jobs with the Navy at the Pearl Harbor Base. Maria worked in the offices at the Naval Hospital, and Adriano got a job as a mechanic at the Red Hill underground gasoline storage facility in Oahu. Like the underground equipment in the mines in Kentucky, he maintained the underground equipment that moved the fuel to the coast and he was a top-notch mechanic with a spotless work record. He enjoyed his work, got promotion after promotion, and they both loved Hawaii.

While they had a happy life, it wasn't the rewarding family life they craved—filled with lots of children. Finally, after extensive medical testing, they learned that Maria did not have any problems that would prevent her from having children. But Adriano did. His sperm counts were just not what they should have been. They were overwhelmed with sadness. That was when fate stepped in in the form of a handsome, ever-charming sailor.

Clarence happened to have shore leave from Ellice Island in the South Pacific in January 1943, and he took it in Hawaii. Not in LA where Ethel and Carolyn were. He was still married to Ethel at this time, but that fact didn't faze him. The island gave him a chance to escape the monotony and endless coral on Funafuti and to be near his old shipmates, whom he still mourned deeply. The Seabees were great guys, but they weren't his lost buddies from the Oklahoma.

Sheer chance brought Maria and Clarence together. She was putting in long hours at work to help her forget that she would never have children. One night, Maria was so worn out, she decided to leave on time and stop for a drink on the way home. That's when she happened to meet Clarence in a Honolulu hotel bar near the base. They were both drinking to forget, he the loss of his buddies, she the fact that she'd never have children. Their eyes sought each other's out and soon they were engrossed in conversation. After a few drinks, they spilled their tales of woe to each other. Maria could empathize with Clarence about loss, after losing her father, her step-father, and especially the loss of a chance at a child. Clarence, being the ever-charming guy that he was, offered to help Maria. He had a room at the hotel, and Clarence and Maria used it effectively.

Before long, she found that she was pregnant. Maria and Adriano were thrilled. Adriano thought the doctors might have missed something, and maybe Hawaii was a charm after all. Maria, of course, knew in her heart where this child came from. In September 1943, Maria delivered a strapping son who they named Ted. He was a handsome little fellow, but Adriano was a bit confused that a blond-haired, blue-eyed baby could be the product of two brown-haired, brown-eyed parents. Although he wasn't a geneticist, Adriano smelled a rat. Maria, of course, knew exactly what was going on.

She told Adriano, "All babies have blue eyes when they're born. As he gets older, Ted's eyes and hair will darken. Then he'll look just like any decent Italian boy."

Adriano was so in love with Maria that he decided he'd let this go for now. And he wondered if it was her Irish ancestry that was coming through. Maybe it skipped a generation? He replied, "Well, I guess you know more about this than I do. But it does seem odd."

After five years, and no perceptible change in Ted's hair or eye colors, Adriano became certain about what he'd long suspected—he'd been cuckolded. So, while Maria got her baby, she lost the love of her life, Adriano. He filed for divorce and moved back to Kentucky. Maria was furious, devastated, and a bit puzzled; she never thought he would react so strongly. Sure, she'd cheated on him once; otherwise she was a model wife. She did give him a child, which apparently, wasn't enough to make him happier. Of course, Ted was another man's child, but she didn't consider that a sufficient reason to warrant a divorce. They had so many other good things going. Finally, she decided that she'd just have to get over it. She'd gotten what she wanted—a child.

Ted grew up to be a healthy, happy boy. He loved his dad Adriano and was saddened by the divorce and losing him. Then, one day when he was about twelve, his mother called to tell him to meet his dad at a Honolulu hotel. Ted was thrilled and looked forward to seeing his father, Adriano, again. He walked into the hotel and looked everywhere, but never found him. Instead, a handsome man in a Navy dress uniform walked up to him and asked if he was Ted. After much confusion and surprise, Ted realized that there was something strange going on. Clarence explained that he was his real father, not Adriano, although he didn't go into any detail about how that happened. Ted spent some time with him, and like everyone, found him to be a charming man (of course).

They enjoyed getting to know one another and met again about two years later.

Ted continued to ask his mother a lot of questions about Clarence. Like Ethel, when faced with Carolyn's questions, she wouldn't talk about him. Maria thought it was important for Ted to meet him, but not at all important for him to know any of the details. He was still a child, after all.

Then Ted reached high school age, and Maria began to worry about the fact that Ted was growing up and might be attracted to non-Caucasian girls. Recalling her family's attitudes, she had no plans for any mixed marriage between her boy and one of "those people," especially Asians. By then, Hawaii wasn't as important a place to her as it once had been, so she shipped herself and Ted back to the continental US, and settled in California, where there were fewer non-Caucasians. She had no intention of going back to Kentucky. Ever.

Like Ethel's Carolyn before him, Ted never really knew his father. While he'd met him a couple of times, that's not like spending time with someone who would be an everyday part of his life. A genetic connection does not make a man a father. Ted always knew that he was not part of a "normal" family, and, like Carolyn, it made him feel like he was weird somehow. While he continued to ask questions, Maria would never talk about Ted's biological father. Although Clarence tried to keep in touch with Maria, which is what led to Ted's meetings with him, Maria was not especially interested in keeping any kind of relationship with him going. To her, he was simply a means to an end and not very important in the grand scheme of things.

Chapter Twenty

Irene, The Woman Who Never Found Mr. Right, but Eventually Found Mr. Wrong

"Finding the right guy for me gets harder & harder,
guess that's why I just stopped trying."
UNKNOWN

Irene. Personal photo.

Irene was born in August 1912, in Philadelphia, on her parents' wedding anniversary. Unlike Ethel and Maria, the first two mothers, she was a big city girl. Like a lot of people from the northeastern part of the country, her family had deep Colonial American ancestry that stretched back to the 1600s, when Thomas Clifton emigrated from England to settle in Delaware. Also, unlike Ethel and

Maria, her family had lived in either Philadelphia or nearby New Jersey for at least 100 years. Her family near in time were not adventurers as Ethel's and Maria's had been.

Those early ancestors eventually made their way from Delaware to New Jersey, and then across the Delaware River to Philadelphia. They included a Revolutionary War Patriot and some seafaring men, including Daniel Baker, who was a river pilot and has a shoal in the Delaware River named after him.

Irene had what to outside appearances seemed to be a good family life, with two loving older brothers, and a mother who adored her, since she was the only girl. Her father and both brothers were members of the Masonic Lodge, and she and her mother belonged to the Order of the Eastern Star, the women's branch of the Masons. As a young girl, she dated young men who belonged to the DeMolay, the youth group of Freemasonry. Nothing clicked with any of them. She looked, but she never found Mr. Right in this group.

Irene's upbringing was very different than Ethel's and Maria's. She came from what was considered a "good" family. Class distinctions divided society then much more than they do now. Her ancestors several generations back traveled in the right social circles, were written up in the New York Times, and although not rich, were far more financially comfortable than most people, especially Irene's immediate family. Having Revolutionary War Patriots and leading citizens in your ancestry was important in Philadelphia, which was extremely class-conscious. Membership in the Masonic Order and the Eastern Star was part and parcel of this.

The only fly in this idyllic ointment was that her father was an alcoholic. Worse, he was an ugly drunk. This led to some bad situations for Irene, especially when she had dates that came to her home to pick her up. Back then, this was the *only* way that nice girls dated young men. Her "Pappy" as she sometimes called him, would confront those young men, and in a slurred voice, demand to know what intentions they had regarding his little girl. She was mortified. The young men were scared off and horribly embarrassed. As a result, there were very few repeat dates.

Despite this, she loved her father dearly. She was his only daughter, and when he wasn't drinking, he doted on her. The one thing she couldn't stand were his binges. She was constantly tasked with dragging him out of the neighborhood Tap Room to bring him back home. As time went on, it began to get very old.

She considered getting out, but, like Ethel and Maria, Irene's family was affected by the Depression. She couldn't bear to think about leaving her mother alone to deal with an alcoholic. Then her father lost his job as a printer and began drinking more than ever. She dropped out of school after the 10th grade to get a job to support the family. Now she began to have some luck, although it wasn't in the romance department. Because she was smart, she managed to land a job at a company called Sharp & Dohme, now Merck, one of the largest pharmaceutical companies in the world.

Irene was good with numbers and worked in the Comptroller's department. Her luck came into play here, too. She loved what she did, and had a wonderful boss, with whom she remained friends for many years. Irene worked at Sharpe & Dohme for fourteen and a half years and had found her home away from home. She developed a routine: working, and dating some, but nothing serious ever developed. Still no Mr. Right. As both of her older brothers got married and moved out, Irene began to wonder if she'd become a spinster.

Then the United States got involved in World War II. Because Irene's family had a long history of military service, all three of the siblings felt the need to do their part. The younger of her two brothers enlisted in the Navy, and the older brother tried to join the Army, but he had a hearing problem that exempted him from service. At that time, the Navy, the Army, and the Air Force all had women's branches; none of them appealed to her. The thought of spending endless days on a rocking ship did not sound good, and she didn't like heights, making the Air Force and planes downright scary. And she just never liked the Army.

The Marine Corps was the last branch of the services to accept women, and when they did, they created the USMCWR—The United States Marine Corps Women's Reserve. Now, *that* sounded pretty swell. The Marine's idea was to recruit women they could train to do non-combat jobs which would free up the men to fight. That was just fine with her. So, she set out to become a lady Leatherneck. She barely made it with one half inch to spare over the 5'1" minimum height requirement.

The other branches of the services had names for the women's corps, like the WACs (Women's Army Corp), the WAVEs (Women Accepted for Volunteer Emergency Service), and the WAFs (Women's Air Force). The Marines never gave in to that. They thought a Marine was a Marine. Perhaps they were ahead of the times when it came to gender equality. The men did have an unofficial name for the female Marines: BAMs, short for Broad-Assed Marines. It was coined by the male Marines, after a female reporter suggested they be called "Beautiful American Marines." Maybe a bit sexist, but definitely memorable. The official word on their name came from Marine Corps General Thomas Holcomb, who was emphatic that the Women Marine reservists were not to be ascribed any sort of nickname. In a March 1944 issue of Life magazine, he announced, "They are Marines. They don't have a nickname and they don't need one. They get their basic training in a Marine atmosphere at a Marine post. They inherit the traditions of Marines. They are Marines."

Irene became a BAM in March 1943. Back then, there was no politically correct term for young women, so they referred to them as the "girls." Those girls also referred to themselves as "Feathernecks," a portmanteau derived from the two words Female and Leathernecks.

She was an early adopter, one of eight women who were the first from the Philadelphia area to join. She was excited and ecstatic, and at the same time, sad and worried to leave her mother.

Irene told her oldest brother in the sternest possible way, "You must swear to me that you'll keep an eye on things and do your best to get and maintain our father on the straight and narrow."

She also lectured her father vigorously before she left, "Now, Pappy, I know you like your bourbon, but I'm not going to be here to haul you out of that tap room. Don't you dare put that burden on my mother."

She was a Marine at heart even before she became one officially. Totally fearless and one take-charge woman.

The Marines are part of the Department of the Navy, and because they had no training facilities for women at that time, they relied heavily on the Navy for basic training for the new female enlistees. They used the U.S. Naval Training School, on the Bronx campus of Hunter College in New York, to get them off on the right foot.

Starting in early 1943, young women from all over the country did their boot camp training there. A small fraction—722 of the first group of 95,000 women—arrived in three waves between March 24th and 26th, and were billeted in nearby apartment houses. Irene was in the first wave. On March 26th, twenty-one platoons, or roughly 600 women Marines, began training. They graduated on April 25th.

Opening of the U.S. Navy recruit camp for WAVES (Women Accepted for Volunteer Emergency Service) at Hunter College (Bronx Campus), New York City (USA), in 1943. At one time in 1944, 5,000 women were training at Hunter College, and a total of 95,000 women volunteers were trained for military service there. Image and caption from Wikimedia commons. Image in the public domain.

Since the school was designed for WAVE indoctrination, the curriculum was largely geared for the Navy. Some subjects were not pertinent for Marines, so modifications were made and reluctant male Marines were pulled from Parris Island to be instructors. Training sessions varied from three and a half to five weeks, and besides the dreaded physical examinations, time was allotted for uniforming, drilling, and physical training. They had lectures on customs and courtesies, history and organization, administration, naval law, map reading, interior guard, defense against chemical attack, defense against air attack, identification of aircraft, and safeguarding military information. It was a lot to cover in such a short time.

Their training was intense. Those "boots," as they called them, worked their buns off from 0530 (5:30 AM) to lights out at 2230 (10:30 PM) every day, with only short breaks for lunch and dinner. For Irene, it was like going to college. And, in fact, she was on a college campus. She had always loved school and having to drop out of high school was painful for her. This training put her right back where she belonged, learning and absorbing like a sponge. She sat on the front row every chance she got and became a favorite of her instructors.

Irene loved the routine and the intellectual stimulation, but her petite stature, at five feet one and one-half inches, gave her some grief during her training. Of course, the women were to be issued uniforms, but because her group was the first, there was no readily available inventory. These included both winter and summer dress uniforms, along with caps, shoes, and blouses. Although the Marines had Lord & Taylor working hard on it, what they eventually got was for taller, larger women, so tiny Irene had to have hers altered significantly, delaying her uniforms' delivery and nearly scuttling her chance at further training.

She did well, finishing in the top of her class. All that hard work and her native intelligence paid off. She was chosen to go to First Sergeant's School. Those Marines were no dummies. They knew a good thing when they saw it. She also picked up a lot of Navy and Marine jargon, like MMRLH, which was posted on envelopes. It meant Marine Mail Rush Like Hell. Once she learned it, it appeared on the bottom of the envelopes for every letter she mailed back home.

Best of all, First Sergeant's School was in Philadelphia, at the U.S. Navy Yard, less than two miles from her family. Although she couldn't stay with them, it was closer than the Bronx, and she had some spare time to spend with her mother and father during that two-month training period. The Marines put their candidates up in the Ben Franklin Hotel, so they had a pretty nice place to stay.

The Clerical School at the Navy Base published a little paper back then called *The Pen & Bayonet*. The troops trained in the Clerical School would go on to become Clerks reporting to a First Sergeant, exactly what Irene and her fellow classmates would become. When she and the other First Sergeant candidates arrived, Irene wrote an article called "Hello, Fellow Marines." In it, she introduced the "girls" and penned a little ditty to be sung to the tune of the Marine Corps hymn that summed up these pioneering women perfectly:

You can tell a girl in the Marines,
You can tell her by her walk.
You can tell a girl in the Marines,
You can tell her by her talk.

You can tell her by her manner,
By her attitude and such.
You can tell a girl in the Marines,
But you cannot tell her much!

In July, Irene became a newly non-commissioned officer—a Sergeant. Her class was composed of seventy-five Marines: sixty-one men, fourteen women. She was one of the first women in the country to obtain that distinction. Irene did it with a final grade of ninety-five. Not bad for a high school dropout. She was in her glory.

Then reality hit. Irene and the thirteen other newly-minted Featherneck Sergeants were assigned to Camp Lejeune in New River, North Carolina, where the heat and humidity were worse than Philadelphia. There was no air conditioning, and the barracks had flying roaches in addition to hot and cold running water. These were the so-called southern tree roaches, not like those smaller, more civilized roaches of the Northern cities that knew their place was on the ground. They had a bad habit of dive-bombing the women while they were in the showers, resulting in a nearly constant barrage of screams. The male Marines thought it was hysterical. The Feathernecks failed to see the humor in it.

In addition to the roaches, there were squadrons of mosquitoes, and platoons of chiggers, which can't be seen, but make you itch like crazy. The Feathernecks arrived in the summer, so they were exposed to the worst that coastal North Carolina could throw at them, with temperatures in the 100-110-degree range, and humidity levels to match.

Camp Lejeune back then was out in the middle of nowhere and was referred to as the "Hell-Hole" by anyone who'd had any experience with it. The reality was worse. It was situated in Onslow County, North Carolina, roughly five miles from the rugged beaches that would be used in training exercises for the Marine Expeditionary Forces. This elite group played a massive role in the Pacific in Guadalcanal and Iwo Jima. Before the Marines came into North Carolina, the area was composed primarily of tenant farms, and many people who lived there still got supplies by boat, just as generations before them had. It was pretty basic.

Irene was used to the environments of Hunter College, the Philadelphia Navy Yard, and the Ben Franklin Hotel. All of them were sophisticated, amenity-filled places to live in. She especially missed the food, which was excellent in those places, and there was lots of it. That wasn't the case in North Carolina, at least not at first. The base was somewhat undeveloped when it was established and built in 1941, and even by 1943, with a population approaching 40,000, it was dramatically different than the near-city it is today, with its 180,000 residents.

Despite that, the "girls" learned to see the positives, and by 1943, the base actually had some decent buildings, all red brick with white trim, so at least it was attractive. One of those buildings was a recreation hall, with dart boards, pool tables, and a dance floor with a jukebox. That contraption seemed to be fixated on one song, "Pistol Packin' Mamma," a 1943 number-one song with words composed by Al Dexter, and it played incessantly. But it was certainly appropriate with all those female Marines, who'd had pistol and rifle training and knew how to shoot as well as pack.

The Marine Corps was also new at this Women Marines game, and when Irene arrived, there were no assigned quarters, and no one appeared to have any idea what she and the other "girls" were supposed to do. They eventually figured it out, and Irene was assigned to the Recruit Depot, responsible for payroll and muster rolls for every group of new recruits who came onto the base.

Muster rolls were registers of the officers and men in a military unit. Back in the 1940s, before computers, it was an avalanche of paperwork, with handwriting and typewriters being the norm for recording data. Just keeping up with the mountains of those records for filing was a

Irene outside the Recruit Depot HQ, Camp Lejeune, North Carolina. Note the sergeant's stripes. Personal photo.

nightmare. Every time a new battalion came in, Irene and her company had to pack up the documents from the previous group and start the process all over again for the new group.

Within a few months, she was promoted to Staff Sergeant, and inherited some men in her company. They got on well, and they loved being "bossed around" by their pipsqueak "Sarge." She settled into her role, and made friends among the troops, both men and women. She also had a good woman Marine friend named Geraldine. Gerry was from Chicago. They met at Hunter College and went through First Sergeant's school together. They were the best of buddies. Gerry even had a car, which they lovingly named "Penny the Passionate Pontiac." Gerry went on to make a career of the Marine Corps and was the first woman Marine to attain the rank of E-9, Master Gunnery Sergeant, in 1960. It was the highest non-commissioned officer rank in the Corps.

In February 1944, Irene was promoted to Tech Sergeant. A Tech or Technical Sergeant was similar in rank to a gunnery sergeant and other technical ranks with which it shared its insignia. Then in March, she made First

Sergeant. By this time, she had 120 women in her company plus nineteen Drill Instructors (DIs)—all men, of course. She developed strong friendships with those DIs, who referred to her as "Top." She learned about leadership and how to get people to do what you want them to do. Within the first year or so of her Marine Corps career, she had racked up an impressive collection of achievements:

- the first woman to leave Sharpe & Dohme to join the Marines
- among the first of eight women to be sworn into the Corps in Philadelphia
- one of the first class of Women Marines to be trained at Hunter College
- among the first group of Women Marines to appear in uniform in Philadelphia
- one of the first group of fourteen chosen from boot camp to attend the inaugural class of Women Marines in First Sergeant's school
- the first of four women to make First Sergeant
- the first woman to replace a male First Sergeant

Life at Camp Lejeune did have its bright spots, and the Feathernecks (along with the Leathernecks) got liberty as long as they behaved. They'd frequently go into the nearest "town," Swansboro, which had a population of 454 in 1940. Not exactly a metropolis. There was a great little restaurant there called Captain Charlie's, where those Yankee girls learned how to eat Southern, from fried green tomatoes to grits to hushpuppies to yummy fried catfish, and crisp, succulent fried chicken. And, it was a change from the base. The locals loved seeing the women Marines, who were still a novelty then. I suspect this is where I learned my love for Southern food, although the only ones I remember my Mom cooking as I was growing up were fried green tomatoes. But I can easily make a meal out of grits. Especially if they have lots of butter and cheese in them.

By August of 1944, there were fewer recruits, so Irene's company began scaling back. They were down from 139 to thirty-seven at this point, and because one of her clerks had been transferred, she was putting in twelve- to eighteen-hour days just trying to keep up. It started to get really old really quickly. The only saving grace was the food on the base was significantly better, and she and Gerry had friends who were cooks and ran the mess hall. So, even when she worked late, she could always get some food, and especially some goodies like cake, brownies, and cookies. Irene loved goodies.

During her time at Camp Lejeune, she met Carl, a fellow Marine who was a Chief Pharmacist's Mate in the Quartermaster Corps. The Quartermasters were responsible for logistics, but served alongside the fighting units so they were in just as much danger. Irene and Carl fell deeply in love. They went to Swansboro and ate great food, along with Gerry and whoever she could round up to go along. Of course, there were several hitches. For one, there was a war going on, so personal planning was complex and uncertain at best. More importantly, Carl had a tricky personal situation. He was married, but separated, when he met Irene, and he was very up-front about it. He swore that he'd soon be divorced, but he said that his wife kept dragging her feet on signing the papers. Irene had finally met who she thought was Mr. Right. If only he was not married. The situation was far from perfect.

They both decided to enjoy life while they could, even if they were in limbo. They had a great time together until he was shipped out, first to San Diego, and then to Iwo Jima. He was in the 5th Division, which was the group that sustained the highest casualties of any Marine Division anywhere in WWII. Irene heard from him sporadically. The last letter she received was in November 1944. She dreaded knowing what that meant, and even pulled some strings to see if she could get any kind of news of him, but to no avail.

Then Irene heard that some of the Women Marines in Camp Lejeune would be going to Hawaii. Irene was thrilled since she and her good friend Gerry were slated to go. They made all sorts of elaborate plans and even did a little skit with their fellow Featihernecks to celebrate. Their outfits of straw skirts and leis topped off with goofy masks and signs that said "Honolulu Here We Come" were the hit of the celebration.

Irene & Gerry in their skit. Personal photos.

Unfortunately, they made plans too soon, and learned that "the Corps" sometimes worked—or didn't work—in mysterious ways. Gerry shipped out in November 1944, leaving poor Irene stuck in North Carolina with the roaches. Finally, in December, just as she was about to have a Christmas leave with her family in Philadelphia, she got orders that she was being shipped to San Diego. That was the first step.

San Diego was a major disappointment to Irene. The Marine Corps base back then was a staging area for the troops going somewhere else, mostly the Pacific. There were waves of them who had to have muster rolls prepared and payroll records initiated, changed, or updated. Unfortunately, her staff there wasn't like the top-notch crew she had at Camp Lejuene. Or as large. And, the constant flow of troops was as never-ending as the California sunshine.

On top of that, Irene was conscientious to a fault. Because of her exceptional experience at Camp Lejuene, and the fact that she excelled at her job, she suspected that the Corps was keeping her from going to Hawaii. Instead of a workload of the two assignments that she handled at Camp Lejeune, she had three in San Diego: one as Acting Sergeant Major; Adjutant (an assistant to the Commanding Officer, or CO); and First Sergeant. Her feelings were likely well-founded. Those responsible were short-handed and they couldn't afford to lose her. She began working twelve- to eighteen-hour days again and started to burn out. Her superiors finally told her to slow down, which she reluctantly did. Meanwhile, her good friend Gerry had shipped off to Pearl Harbor, so she didn't even have a buddy to gripe and share late-night snacks with.

Eventually the workload lightened up significantly, and life got easier in San Diego, so Irene could enjoy a bit of time to herself. She made one weekend trip up to Los Angeles with some other Feathernecks so she could see first-hand what Hollywood was all about. They went to The Brown Derby, Sardi's, the legendary Clifton's Cafeteria, and saw Grauman's Chinese Theater with its celebrity footprints and handprints. In spite of its supposed glamour, she wasn't impressed with Hollywood, and thought it seemed like any other smallish town. Irene was a big city girl, after all.

Right at home in San Diego, the Marine Corps base had occasional dances, which she thought were much more fun than Hollywood, and she went to as many of them as she could. At least they were easier to get to, and less expensive. Best of all, they played a bigger variety of songs than "Pistol-Packin Mamma." There were new tunes too, like "Ac-Cent-Tchu-Ate the Positive" that she could jitterbug to and "Sentimental Journey" for those dreamy slow dances.

Among her other duties, Irene scheduled the Marines who were on her muster rolls for physicals and dental checkups before they shipped out, so she had frequent contacts with those who were responsible for scheduling at those facilities. Clarence was now stationed at the Dental Clinic in San Diego, performing duties as a Dental Technician, and one of his responsibilities was scheduling. They spoke to each other frequently by phone. For weeks, in addition to setting appointments, they laughed and joked and engaged in some serious flirting with one another.

On one occasion, Clarence told Irene, "I heard you need to have all your teeth pulled. I'm so sorry to hear that, but

I'm just the guy to be the technician to assist when you get that done."

Irene was pretty clever too, so she shot back at him, "Listen, buster, if you even think about doing that, I'll send a platoon of my Marine buddies over to rough you up."

They both enjoyed the verbal foreplay and worked hard at coming up with more outlandish things to tell each other.

In between the joking, Clarence was flattering her, telling her, "I just love working with you. You're so efficient, and you have the nicest voice. It's always a pleasure to talk to you. Maybe someday, we can get some coffee so I can see if you look as pretty as you sound?"

Irene was flattered and took his compliments graciously. And, she liked the idea of a guy with a good sense of humor. She was used to bantering and teasing, with two older brothers who were constantly playing tricks on her as they were growing up.

By this time, Irene had given up on Carl, fearing he was lost in the fierce fighting on Iwo Jima. Eventually, Clarence skipped past the coffee, and asked Irene to meet him at the NCO (Non-Commissioned Officers) Club for dinner. He was still handsome, still ever so charming—and still married to Ethel. But Irene didn't know that. And, of course, she never knew about Maria and that little blond-haired, blue-eyed Italian boy of hers. Clarence even told Irene that he'd written to his mother about her. A bold-faced lie if ever there was one. Unfortunately, there was no way Irene could know that. Clarence's mother had visited California back in the "good days" of his marriage to Ethel, so if he'd written to her about Irene, she would know something was not right with his marriage, and he'd have been caught out.

Free to fib, Clarence told Irene one night at dinner, "I really enjoy being with you, Irene. You're smart, and fun and pretty. I'd like to start seeing you on a regular basis."

Irene was pleased with that, saying, "I'd like that too, but I don't want us to get too serious too soon. With this war going on, who knows where we might end up?"

That was music to Clarence's ears. They continued to see each other regularly, and the relationship deepened. On Irene's side, she hoped it might lead to something long-term. On Clarence's, Irene was just another pretty woman who he could win over. Eventually, this strong, decisive woman gave in to his advances.

Meanwhile, up in Los Angeles, Ethel decided she'd had as much as she wanted to stand with her philandering husband. She began talking to lawyers and starting the process of divorcing Clarence.

Back on the work front, Irene's performance and dedication were officially recognized, and she was finally put up for promotion to Sergeant Major. It was long overdue. She'd been acting in that capacity for six and a half months. During this time, her CO came to call her "Boss."

In June 1945, Irene got the news she'd been dreading. No more transfers to Hawaii. That meant the staging area would close soon. She had no idea what would happen to her or where she'd go. In late August, after the bombing of Hiroshima, her promotion was finally effective. After Hiroshima, she understood with wise foresight that the war would soon end, and that Hawaii would be a no-go. Once again, the Corps worked in strange ways, and just after the Japanese surrendered on September 2nd, her orders for Hawaii arrived. Timing, in this case, was every-thing. Those orders came in a day *after* the last ship sailed.

And, with the surrender came word that the Women's Reserve would demobilize. Her Marine Corps career was over.

At that time, the Marines had a point system in place that was based on longevity and rank. It allowed those Women's Reservists with sufficient points to apply for an immediate discharge. It helped the Corps, since they weren't quite sure what to do with all those women, and it helped the women, who had to think hard about what to do with themselves now that the war was over. Irene decided to take them up on it.

Unlike those who served for twenty years or more, Irene and the other short-timers got nothing for their service except a final paycheck, a pat on the back for a job well done, and a lifetime of stories they could tell their families and children.

Like everything else in the military, there was a torturous process that she had to go through to get her discharge, including a physical exam. She completed all her paperwork and submitted it and was scheduled for her physical.

After a brief, but thorough exam, the doctor told her, "You're in excellent physical condition. Your lab results show that you have low blood sugar, good cholesterol levels, and normal hemoglobin. The only thing I might recommend is to lose some weight." As he said this he smiled and told her, "But, you should probably wait until after your baby is born to do that."

Irene was flabbergasted when she heard that news. She thought those fourteen pounds she'd gained were just from too much good eating and the stress of working so hard. One thing she knew for sure was that Clarence was the culprit. Although she'd seen other guys while she was in San Diego, Clarence was the only one she'd "known" in the Biblical sense. She told him the news. Then she found out he was married. Of course, he didn't tell her that his wife was about to file for divorce. That would have put him on the spot. And, he had something else going on that Irene didn't know about: a long-term liaison with a woman who would later turn out to be the fifth and final mother, Angelina.

Irene was overcome with a barrage of emotions, from anger at herself for being so vulnerable and giving in so easily to Clarence's charms, to anxiety and uncertainty about what she should do. Like Ethel, she decided that Clarence was a bastard of the first magnitude. She was also deeply ashamed of the position she was in, and the shame that it would bring to her and to her family. "Nice" girls from good families in Philadelphia just didn't do things like that back then.

Shortly before Irene was discharged, "Mr. Right," Carl, came back from Iwo Jima. He was one of the lucky ones to have survived. He, too, turned out to be a major disappointment.

He told Irene, "My wife is still not agreeing to a divorce, and I've decided to go back home to try to work things out. It's the least I can do to try to save what's left of my marriage."

Aside from that, Irene in no way wanted to saddle him with someone else's child. They never saw each other again.

By now, she was completely convinced that all men, except maybe her brothers, were dirty rotten scoundrels, and vowed never, ever to become involved with one again. Until the end of her life, she kept that vow, and didn't date or have any relationships beyond friendship with a man.

Meanwhile, she had to decide what to do and where to go next. Fortunately, Irene had a good Marine buddy who was living in Los Angeles, so once all of her paperwork was cleared, and her discharge was final, she temporarily moved in with her and her husband. Then she found out about the Florence Crittenton Home.

The Crittenton organization was founded by an evangelist, whose mission was to establish local homes for the care of "fallen women" and their children. The Los Angeles home was established in 1892. The Crittenton Home became Irene's home.

The Crittendon Home. With the exception of Camp Lejeune, Irene managed to end up in some pretty nice digs, even under difficult circumstances. Personal photo.

In January 1946, I arrived. Irene named me after two of her Marine Corps buddies, Mary, the name of her CO in San Diego, and Jo, one of her close friends from Camp Lejeune.

Irene swore that she'd protect her little girl from all the bad things in the world, especially men. From the time I was old enough to start noticing boys—at about twelve—my mom warned me of how boys would do whatever they could to get them to give into things good girls shouldn't do. But, she never really talked in detail about what those things were, only that they'd try to snag a feel and get her pants down. My sex education, like most girls' in those days, was sadly lacking.

More importantly, now Irene had someone in her life who could do the things she had never accomplished, like graduating from high school and "making something of herself." I've never been able to understand this about my mom. She had accomplished so much in her life that very few women might have been able to do. In spite of all her achievements in the Marine Corps, which were signify-cant, she apparently always felt she could have done more. She was a classic over-achiever, constantly thinking that what she'd done could and should have been more.

It took years, and writing this book, to make me realize the enormity of what my mom had accomplished. She was truly a trailblazer. For years, she hid her light under a bushel, and it was only in her later years that she shared of lot of her Marine Corps history with me. I am still as-tounded by what she did and know now why I was able to be as successful as I have been. Thanks, Mom.

Her challenge was to figure out what to do next. After staying in LA for three months, she decided to go back home to Philadelphia. She didn't really like California, and she missed her family terribly. Her beloved mother had developed rheumatoid arthritis, and in those days, treat-ment for this debilitating, disabling disease was non-existent. Because she was no longer able to walk, they set up a bed and a big easy chair for her in their living room. That room would become the center of her existence for the next eighteen years. Rheumatoid arthritis crippled, but it didn't kill you. It just made you miserable and next to impossible to get around or do anything for yourself. Irene went back home to care for her.

Obviously, I went along. It seemed to be the perfect solution. Irene had her new mission, and it would provide a wonderful, loving home with a multi-generational family in which her child could be happy and grow and prosper.

Irene with 3-month old Mary Jo
in Philadelphia. Personal photo

Clarence, meanwhile, was divorced by Ethel. After San Diego, he spent a short amount of time in Hawaii, and met mother number four—Yoshiko.

Chapter Twenty-One

Yoshiko, Number Four

"If a relationship has to be a secret, you shouldn't be in it."
RITU GHATOUREY

Yoshiko, iStock photo.

Yoshiko was born in March 1924 in Oahu, Hawaii. For those of you who get confused about the Hawaiian Islands, as I do, trying to figure out which one is which, Oahu is where the Pearl Harbor Naval Base, and Honolulu, the state's capital, are located. Despite what you might think, it is not the "big" island. That's where the cool volcanoes are.

Yoshiko's family originally came from Hiroshima, Japan, when her grandfather, Kenta, and one of his brothers left their family's farm in 1866 after a series of crop failures nearly wiped their households out. The Waialua

Sugar Company was recruiting men in Japan, promising good wages if they came to Hawaii to work for them and a chance to make some money they could send back to their families. Unfortunately, those recruits soon learned that the price of Waialua's good money was extremely harsh working conditions, with twelve- to fifteen-hour days of backbreaking physical labor. The even harsher environment and economic conditions in Japan drove them to sign up. Otherwise, their families might starve. Like many of his fellow workers, Kenta and his brother had three-year contracts. Unlike his brother and half of those he came with, he stayed on at the end of his contract, bringing over the sister of one of his good friends from Hiroshima and marrying her. Kenta was a long-term thinker and was determined not to be a quitter.

Kenta and his bride Haruko had three children—two girls and a boy, Ichiro. Ichiro grew up strong and smart, and worked on the sugar plantation like his father. Besides being hard working, he was shrewd, and knew he could do more than the exhausting work his father did day after day. Ichiro volunteered for extra shifts when the bosses were shorthanded, finished his work early so he could lend them a hand, and did whatever it took to be noticed favorably and make their jobs easier. Those bosses did notice. Over time, he was promoted to increasingly better jobs, and eventually, earned a supervisory position, which provided a comfortable life for his family, far better than the life his father had. His parents had lived in company housing near the pineapple fields so Kenta could be closer to work. It was almost like the company town in Kentucky, Lynch, where Maria had grown up, with its company housing and stores. Ichiro and his wife, Akemi, had a large private home and a car to get around the island in, and they planned for a large family.

Unlike attitudes on the US mainland, the Japanese in Hawaii were not systematically treated as potential traitors during World War II. In fact, many young Japanese, whose families had lived on the islands for generations, served in either the Army's 442nd Regimental Combat Team, or the All-Hawaii 100th Infantry Battalion. By this time, the 157,000 Japanese made up about a third of the Hawaiian Islands' population, and fewer than 1,800 of them were placed in internment camps.

It was a very different story on the mainland. Roughly 120,000 people out of a Japanese population of 127,000 were interned in ten camps across the US. Many of those camps were in remote locations, far from the cities where Japanese immigrants and US citizens of Japanese descent lived. Of those interred, sixty two percent were US citizens. Part of the reason for the low internment rate in Hawaii may be that the Japanese workers were critical to the sugar cane and pineapple plantations' operations, whose owners were politically and economically powerful.

Those who were interned were either prominent in the community or thought to be some sort of risk. Unfortunately, Ichiro's job put him in that prominent category, and he and his family were terrified that they might be put in a camp. They had good reason to feel that way, since entire families were interned, not just those who were considered to be disloyal or a risk to national security. Fortunately, at the last minute, Ichiro's boss and the head of the sugar plantation campaigned hard and vouched for his loyalty. Economics and political clout won out, and they were spared.

Ichiro and his wife, Akemi, tried for years to have children. Just when they thought they might never have any, Akemi became pregnant and gave birth to a beautiful baby girl, who they named Yoshiko. The name Yoshiko means "Good Child" in Japanese, and since Ichiro was in his forties when she was born, she became his little adored one. She was a beautiful child, with coal-black hair that always had a near-metallic sheen from repeated brushing, and mischievous brown eyes that sparkled in the sun.

Ichiro's wife, Akemi, was a wonderful mother, although not as obsessed as Ichiro was with their child. From the time she was a baby, Ichiro treated Yoshiko like a princess, doing whatever he had to do to give her the things he thought she should have. It was an idyllic life for a little girl. She fit well into the Japanese community on Oahu, had a lot of friends, and enjoyed the social status of a child whose father was a supervisor rather than a lower-paid and lower-status laborer. But her mother kept her grounded, so she was not a spoiled brat. She went to beach parties, learned to surf and fish, and loved any kind of outdoor activity. Hawaii's climate made that easy for her.

For her sixteenth birthday, Ichiro and Akemi arranged for an immense beach party luau. From their Japanese roots, they had sushi, sashimi, and tempura. Because this was Hawaii, they honored (and loved) Hawaiian customs and food. There was a whole roasted pig, poi, a paste of boiled and pounded taro roots mixed with water, and poke, a dish made from raw fish marinated in lime juice, with green onions, chili peppers, sea salt, soy sauce, sesame oil, roasted macadamia nuts, and seaweed. To accompany these, there were purple Hawaiian sweet potatoes, and taro rolls for making sandwiches with that juicy, savory, slow-roasted pork. Of course, there were pineapple dishes galore for dessert. For entertainment, Ichiro even hired a slack-key guitar player.

Yoshiko had a contented childhood and did well in school. She loved her science classes, particularly biology. Her talents and enjoyment led her to volunteer at Queen's Medical Center during high school. She enjoyed those experiences so much that she applied to and entered their nursing program after graduation. As she did throughout high school, she excelled in nursing school and stayed on at Queen's for several years before getting a position at Aiea Naval Hospital in 1947. That was where she met Clarence. He was serving as a Chief Pharmacist's Mate that year, after his divorce from Ethel, but before he married the fifth and final mother, Angelina. He really was a free man then.

Unlike some of the nurses she worked with, Yoshiko was not at all interested in sailors, and Clarence still harbored suspicions about the Japanese after the loss of his buddies on the Oklahoma in Pearl Harbor. Both of their opinions changed over time. They began to get to know one another when Yoshiko needed an emergency drug—sulfapyridine—for one of her dangerously ill patients who had developed septicemia. She and the doctors knew that the drug would work wonders and likely save their patient's life. Yoshiko had no idea what the impact of meeting Clarence would have on her. Although she did know that her family would look with disfavor on a relationship with an American sailor, so she didn't really consider him a romantic match, but merely a mild flirtation. What harm could that be?

Yoshiko was expected to find and marry a good Japanese boy from a prominent family, and she was not averse to that plan either. But there was just something about that pill-pusher fella that she found interesting. For starters, he always looked swell, and he was a great conversationalist.

They started out having coffee in the hospital cafeteria, where he told her stories of his childhood in Kentucky. She was fascinated with the idea of snow and hoped that someday she might experience it first-hand. Being an only child, she couldn't imagine having seven brothers and sisters, as Clarence did, and enjoyed hearing about their adventures in the woods when he was a boy. They both loved fishing and swapped endless fish stories.

Clarence told her, "My brothers and I would fish in Bear Creek and would catch a basket full of huge bass that would feed the whole family. Fortunately, our family loved fish!"

Yoshiko topped this, saying, "Well, I learned to surf fish from my dad, and caught baskets full of monster-sized fish. One of those fish was a shark, and it was taller than I am. At first, I thought it was a mermaid. I brought it in all alone." Yoshiko could tell a tall tale. Clarence had met his match and loved it.

The coffees soon progressed to fishing dates and then to lunches and dinners, where they had to be careful of where they met, for fear of her parents finding out. They frequented small restaurants, and even went to little shacks on the beach that served up delicious shrimp and fish dishes—and anonymity. Of course, her family knew nothing about their clandestine meetings. They would have been horrified and furious.

As time went on, she became more than mildly interested in Clarence, enjoying his charm and his stories more than she wanted to admit—even to herself. Several of her nursing friends at the hospital tried to warn her about Clarence. They'd had much more experience with swabbies than she did and knew a philanderer when they saw one. As might be expected, despite their best efforts, Yoshiko's and Clarence's relationship progressed to its logical conclusion. Sex was always Clarence's end game and he'd perfected it for years.

Yoshiko, like Ethel and Irene, soon discovered that she was eating for two. After a month of almost debilitating morning sickness, she realized she was pregnant and had no idea what to do. She had to tell her parents, who were enraged over her indiscretion, and threw her out of the house. She was disappointed in herself for giving in to Clarence so easily, but, more importantly, mortified at bringing shame to her family.

Fortunately, like Irene, she found a safe haven called the Mary Jane Home. Run by the Catholic diocese of Hawaii, it offered Yoshiko shelter away from her family, and the option to put the baby up for adoption after birth. She stayed there the entire length of her pregnancy, helping the other young mothers-to-be with her nursing skills. She never told Clarence anything about it, just that she was leaving the hospital for a chance at a better job on the mainland. That's what her family told everyone, too. She was dead to them.

Delivery pains for Yoshiko were excruciating. They discovered that the baby boy was in the breech position, with his legs coming out first. Obstetrics then was not what it is today, and although the doctors and nurses struggled hard to turn that baby around, they couldn't manage it. Yoshiko died during labor, but gave birth to a healthy little boy. Like all those who stayed in the Mary Jane Home, she'd made arrangements for the baby to be adopted after birth, and he was whisked off to the orphanage run by Catholic Social Services in Honolulu. The full-blooded Japanese, Hawaiian, and American babies were easily adopted out of the orphanage; mixed-race babies were a harder group to place. Yoshiko's boy was one of them, with a Japanese mother and an American father. That cute, tiny boy stayed there for four long years.

After all that time, fate stepped in and two angels from the mainland adopted this little child with the winning smile and twinkling eyes that were mildly Japanese-looking. He likely inherited his eyes from Yoshiko and some of that charm from Clarence. They were thrilled to find him and didn't care a bit about his mixed ancestry. They named him Victor Rodney, an odd name for a half-Japanese, half-American child, but his adoptive mother, Johanna, was of German descent, so Victor Rodney it was. They called him Rodney.

Johanna was raised in Milwaukee, Wisconsin, and worked as an anesthesiologist in the VA Hospital in St. Louis. That's where she met Rodney's dad, who was a Japanese veteran from Hawaii. He served in the Army's All-Hawaii Company, 100th Infantry Battalion, in Europe, whose motto was "Remember Pearl Harbor." This group was famous for their exploits in Italy, particularly at Monte Cassino, where they faced and defeated the Germans. It's said that after that battle, generals fought among themselves for these men to be part of their troop command. The All-Hawaii became the most decorated military unit in American history. So much for those Japanese not being loyal to the US.

Rodney, of half-Japanese, half-American descent, took his father's name, Tanaka, after his adoption. Perhaps because of his adopted father's military service, and unknowingly, his birth father's career, he went on to become part of a US Navy Underwater Demolition Seal team in Vietnam. This was the beginning of the Seals, established by President John F. Kennedy in 1962 as a small, elite maritime military force to conduct unconventional warfare. Rodney's training group graduated thirty-six men out of a starting base of 150. He was nicknamed "Pineapple" by his Seal buddies because of his Hawaiian heritage.

———————◦———————

While Rodney waited in that orphanage to be adopted, Clarence completed his stint in Hawaii and moved on to Guam. He couldn't wait to finish his assignment there. He knew that Angelina was waiting in the wings for him, in San Francisco.

Chapter Twenty-Two

Angelina, The Woman
Who Turned the Tables

"There is an old and very wise Native American saying: Every time you point a finger in scorn—there are three remaining fingers pointing right back at you."
ALYSON NOEL, FATED

Angelina. Personal photo.

Angelina was born in 1917 in San Antonio, Texas to a Mexican-American family. Both of her parents had emigrated from Mexico, and she was one of three children, all born in the United States. Because most older, non-US public record-keeping is sparse, and tends to favor those from wealthy families or with some degree of political standing, very few details are known about her forbears in Mexico. From Mexican and US census, naturalization, and death records, we know that her father worked for a time as a barber, and then as a roofer in building construction, in San Antonio. His father, before him, was a teacher in Mexico. The family came from Guanajuato, Mexico. They all became naturalized citizens.

Angelina was lucky to be born in the US, compared to her parents, who came to Texas to improve their lives and those of their children. She was born into a culturally-rich Mexican-American community in San Antonio, where bilingual English/Spanish was the norm and Mexican cultural traditions were alive and well. They continue to be to this day, making San Antonio a great place to visit and experience the traditions there.

San Antonio has a rich history, starting as the first civilian settlement in Texas. Originally called San Antonio de Béxar, it was founded in 1718. Its history stretches back to the establishment of five missions in the early 1700s, when the Spanish moved up from Mexico into what was then called Coahuila y Tejas, an amalgamation of parts of Mexico and what is now Texas. Following the early Spaniards, German immigrants moved into Texas in the 1800s and became some of the early landowners and merchants. This just added to the already-rich diversity there.

Its best-known Spanish mission, although many non-Texans don't know that it was a mission, is The Alamo. Originally named San Antonio de Valero, it is the site of the failed, but hard-fought stand in 1836 against Santa Ana and his Mexican troops, where virtually all of the Texians, including Davy Crockett, were killed. Although Santa Ana won this battle, a month later he was completely overwhelmed at the battle of San Jacinto near Houston, where the rallying cry among the troops was "Remember the Alamo!" In 1845, Texas became part of the United States. It is a place and culture defined by war, from its beginnings through the world wars and beyond. Angelina was affected by that climate, with a strongly developed sense of patriotism and a willingness to fight for what she believed in.

Angelina didn't care about any of this historical sweep as a child growing up. And her immediate environment in the 1930s was not nearly as grand as that once experienced by Teddy Roosevelt at The Menger Hotel, when he was there to recruit his legendary Rough Riders for the Spanish-American War. She lived in an area of Mexican immigrants, where people struggled on a daily basis to make ends meet. Luckily for Angelina and her family, and unlike Ethel's and Maria's families, Texas was not Kansas or Kentucky. Although the depression hit there, too, there was no dust bowl in that part of Texas. Plus, her parents were used to struggling. It was just more of the same.

The sub-tropical Texas climate at least allowed people to grow some food year-round, so survival was a little easier. And Mexican-Americans know how to make food stretch, with dishes like tamales, enchiladas, and beans filling tummies. Family dinners were frequent and were always a noisy affair, with *abuelos* (grandfathers), *abuelas* (grandmothers), *tias* (aunts), *tios* (uncles), and scores of *primos* (cousins) bringing food and sharing their stories with one another. They talked about their lives, they talked about their children, and they talked about their grandchildren once they had them. Angelina's family loved babies, and oohed and ahhed over every new one that entered their large family. Angelina wasn't so sure. Of course, she liked babies and children, but she wasn't convinced that she wanted a lot of them. She didn't want to be tied down.

One of the dishes her family loved was a soup called menudo. It's made with tripe, the lining of a cow's stomach, and what Anglos call hominy, dried maize kernels which have been treated with lye. While it sounds terrible, it's very tasty. Menudo is flavored with cilantro and oregano or marjoram, with a dash of heat from jalapenos, and is savory as well as spicy. The belief is that menudo is a great hangover cure, so it served two purposes. And it still does. It's popular among Mexicans, especially on Sundays, after a long night on Saturday.

For Angelina as a child, growing up in that environment was a wonderful experience, with a lot of family togetherness and great food. But it also had its downsides. Because families were so close, everyone knew everyone else's business, and if a young person had an independent streak, it could be stifling. Angelina started life with a strong sense of independence. When she was very young and just learning to speak, she showed that by insisting that she do things herself, often proclaiming: "I do, I do." And that sense of independence only grew stronger as she got older.

Once she matured into her teenage years, her family began to constantly tell her what she should and shouldn't do, and with whom she should associate. They even had a boy they'd earmarked for her, a handsome lad named Julio whose parents owned a furniture store. Her family knew that an association with him would bring her a comfortable life and a rung up on the social ladder. Although Julio was quite stricken with Angelina, she wanted no part of him. She'd make her own choice, thank you.

She was a beauty, with long, wavy dark hair and sparkling mischievous eyes that attracted a lot of boys—not just Julio. That was her idea of a good time, not being stuck with just one. While her kind of beauty was the norm in San Antonio, Angelina liked to be different. After she finished high school, she decided that San Antonio was tolerable, but she didn't want to spend the rest of her life there. And, she had no intention of getting married.

She often said to anyone who would listen, "I have no plans to marry a Mexican and have a boatload of kids. My goal is to have fun, especially with the boys. A lot of boys."

After she graduated from high school, she worked at Frost Brothers, San Antonio's elite downtown department store, in the cosmetic department. She was pretty enough to attract the men to buy perfume and had an eye for makeup to sell a lot to the women. Angelina saved up enough money to get to San Francisco, where an aunt and some cousins lived. She got a job there in the Gimbels department store, made a lot of friends at work, and began going out to dances at the USO. There were always a lot of handsome sailors and Marines at those dances who had come up from San Diego on weekend passes. That was where she met Clarence.

Angelina and Clarence met in early 1941, before he was married to Ethel. He told her tales of his Navy adventures, and she ate them up. He was, after all, a handsome, charming man. Best of all, he wasn't Mexican. So, Angelina encouraged the relationship. True to her roots, Angelina made a mean menudo, and Clarence learned to enjoy it. He was consistently "cured" by it on Sundays after a night of heavy drinking.

They saw each other occasionally when Clarence got to San Francisco until Clarence and Ethel got married in that shotgun wedding in April of 1941. But, their relationship didn't stop completely; they still saw each other sporadically. They soon discovered they were kindred spirits.

They both liked to drink, and they both wanted adventure and excitement. Without any strings.

Their on and off relationship continued through Clarence's marriage to Ethel in LA, his gracious offer to Maria in Pearl Harbor, his short-lived dalliance with Irene, and his fling with Yoshiko. There was just something there with Angelina that kept him coming back. Aside from the sex, Clarence was passionate about talking to Angelina, sharing his feelings of loss at his buddy's deaths in Pearl Harbor, and regaling her with tales of his time with the Seabees in Funafuti and the South Pacific. Angelina loved listening, and she loved Clarence deeply. Not just for the sex. She loved just being with him and talking to him. She knew he was married, but she also knew it had been a forced marriage and that he wasn't happy. That was her justification.

After Ethel's divorce from Clarence was finalized in August 1946, he became a free man. Then something else happened to him. At the ripe old age of twenty-seven, he was finally starting to grow up. He stopped drinking, his work performance improved, and he was getting advancements in the Navy. He also decided to stay single for a while. After all he'd experienced, he was beginning to wonder if women were more trouble than they were worth, especially if you married them. He decided that dealing with so many women might be more trouble than it was worth. Of all the women he had known so far, Angelina was the most comfortable fit for a marriage where he could be himself. Of course, his sex drive didn't stop, as evidenced by his fling with Yoshiko in Hawaii. Regardless, Angelina was always there, listening, compliant, and not trying to push him into anything permanent. It was a perfect situation.

In 1947, Clarence was transferred to Fleet Marine Force Headquarters in Hawaii, then to the 5th Service Depot in Guam. In July of that year, he re-enlisted. He'd decided by that time that the Navy was providing him with a good career. He was also getting good conduct medals rather than the AOLs he'd racked up in his earlier years. He accrued fifty days' leave, and in February 1948, decided to take it in San Francisco, where Angelina was still living and waiting for him.

Clarence and Angelina were delighted to be together again, and after giving it a lot of thought, he decided that being married to Angelina might not be a bad thing. He loved just being with her. Angelina enjoyed their "no strings attached" relationship, and she wasn't so sure about being tied to one man. Although it took some doing, he managed to convince her to marry him. She truly did love him, so after a lot of persuasive arguments from Clarence, she finally gave in. They tied the knot on February 29th, 1948 while he was on leave. They took the leap in a leap year. Her mother and her aunts back in San Antonio were thrilled. Their Angelina was finally settling down. Now all they needed was some babies.

In April, Clarence was reassigned to the First Marine Aircraft Wing in Santa Ana, south of LA. Angelina went with him, of course. She didn't like LA as much as she loved San Francisco, but at least it was still California. Then in November 1949, he was transferred to the Naval Air Station in Memphis, Tennessee. By now, Angelina was getting her share of travel. And she was loving it. Life being married to a Navy guy allowed her to see a lot more of the country than San Antonio.

Angelina wasn't so sure about that transfer to Memphis, since she'd come to love California. Like Clarence, she was always up for some kind of adventure and fun, so she went into it with an open mind. Then she got there and discovered that people in that part of the country talked funny. Despite the fact that Memphis was diverse when it came to Caucasians and African-Americans, many of them didn't like Mexicans. Those Memphians would whisper behind their backs, refuse to eat near them in restaurants, and considered them only good for yard work and cleaning their homes.

The only saving grace was that Angelina and Clarence lived on the base, so she quickly developed friendships with the other Navy wives. They spoke "normally" and didn't have anything against Mexicans. She settled into a happy married existence, with Clarence by her side, and a lot of Navy wives for friends. She decided that marriage might be okay after all. Maybe she had worried too much about being tied down. Or maybe her independent streak was waning.

In February 1951, Clarence and Angelina were blessed with the love of their hearts, a little girl who they named Elizabeth, or Liz for short. She was a smiling, bouncy baby, and soon totally captivated both of them. Liz was the first of the children of those silent mothers to be born into something like a normal family. She had both a mom and a dad, and they were always there for her. After all of her protests, Angelina became a fine mother once she had that beautiful baby girl with her dark curly hair. She began to understand why her family loved babies so much.

By now, Clarence was securely ensconced in his role of a Dental Assistant. He re-enlisted again and was transferred from the Naval Air Station in Memphis to the *USS Bryce Canyon*, which was berthed at the time in San Francisco. Angelina was delighted. She'd get back to

California and finally get away from those southerners who talked like they had a mouth full of grits. And, it would be good to get their daughter out of the South and back to "normalcy" in California. Their move went well, and in June 1953, Clarence and Angelina completed their perfect family with a baby boy who they named Edward and called little Eddie.

Clarence stayed in the Navy for a few more years and became a model husband and father. He loved both their kids dearly. When they got old enough, and as soon as the New York Giants relocated to San Francisco, he took them to baseball games. Liz and Eddie are still big Giants fans to this day. He carried them on his shoulders, first one, then the other in turn, and bought them hot dogs and Cracker Jacks at the games. And he taught them how to cheer their team on. They all had a ball.

Since Clarence loved to fish and bowl, he took them fishing and bowling with him. Liz and Eddie both learned to love bowling as much as their dad, and they got pretty good at it. In later years, Liz even bowled in a league with her work buddies. Eddie decided that he preferred fishing, and to this day, enjoys camping and fishing with his family.

Finally, in June 1957, Clarence retired from nearly 20 years in the Navy to inactive duty with the Naval Reserve. By that time, he was a Dental Technician Supervisor. It took him a while, but eventually he did well for a wild, undisciplined boy from Kentucky. After the Navy, he went to work for Pacific Gas & Electric, at the Feather River hydroelectric plant. He started settling into and enjoying civilian life.

Now Angelina had him full time, something she wasn't used to. Over the next two years, their relationship became increasingly strained. He was always there, something that Angelina found annoying. Clarence constantly got under her feet and thought he should run the household. Angelina, with her strong independent streak, was accustomed to doing that herself, so she began to resent him. Her resentment turned to anger, and they started to fight constantly. Those fights did not provide a good environment for the passionate encounters they were used to when Clarence was only home sporadically. He was used to a partner who was always there and ready for his advances.

Finally, in an ironic twist of fate, she began cheating on him. The man who ran around on women nearly his entire early life went ballistic and filed for divorce in 1959. He knew that he had strong desires; he didn't realize that Angelina's were that strong. He had even changed for her, not drinking heavily any longer and doing his best to be a model husband and father. Look what that got him. The obvious thing to do was to start to drink again.

This was hard on Clarence, but it was particularly hard on the kids. Liz was nine and Eddie was seven. Unlike Carolyn, Ted, and Mary Jo, they knew what it was like to have a father. By the time they were born, Clarence was finally a pretty decent one. So, to lose him came as a blow to them.

Angelina understood to a degree, but she'd never admit that to Clarence. She was mad as a hornet, and she had quite a temper. She eventually married the guy she was cheating with, leaving Liz and Eddie with a step-father. As with Carolyn, it wasn't like having their own dad. They missed him horribly and they constantly asked Angelina about him. But, just like Ethel, Maria, and Irene, she wouldn't talk about him. She didn't think badly of him;

she just didn't think their relationship was something to share with her children.

Angelina became the last in a string of women who'd known and loved Clarence. As my half-siblings and I now know, they were also what we began to call The Silent Mothers. Despite our best attempts, they would never talk about him. This completely frustrated us, and ultimately killed our ability to know about half of our reason for being in the world. And, for me, it likely meant the end of my search for tracking the root of my medical mystery, familial tremor.

Part Four

The Kids' Paths

"There is divine beauty in learning... To learn means to accept the postulate that life did not begin at my birth. Others have been here before me, and I walk in their footsteps. The books I have read were composed by generations of fathers and sons, mothers and daughters, teachers and disciples. I am the sum total of their experiences, their quests. And so are you."
ELIE WIESEL

Chapter Twenty-Three

Oh, the Fifties Were a Wonderful Time, Weren't They?

"Nothing has a stronger influence psychologically on their environment and especially on their children than the unlived life of the parent."
CARL JUNG

So much has been written about this era that many people who are living today and didn't experience it think of it as a simpler time that was filled with rainbows, happiness and good things. Service men and women were returning from World War II and Korea. Many of the men were going to college on the GI Bill.

They bought homes in suburbs like Levittown, where they could realize The American Dream of owning a single-family house. Levittown was one of the first housing developments—or subdivisions as we call them now. The developers were ahead of their time, providing many amenities, like community centers and pools. The homes were moderately priced, thanks to the use of assembly line-like building techniques, and required a low-down payment, making them affordable to those returning GIs. Of course, their homes all had a perfectly manicured green lawn, and a garage big enough for their new Chevy or Ford. For those people, it probably was good. But, there was a dark side to Levittown too. They did not sell to African Americans. Despite what many people think, the North was not a bastion of racial equality in those days.

The Levittowner

PRICE: $10,990 $67 A MONTH

NO CASH REQUIRED FROM VETERANS

An Example of a Levittown home. From The State Museum of Pennsylvania and the Levittown Library. Copyright owner unknown. Levitt & Sons filed for bankruptcy in 2007.

Even some individuals who lived through it and didn't experience those good times still think fondly of it. You see it all the time on Facebook and Pinterest, where people share their memories of magical things like rotary phones, carhops, and DA (Duck's Ass) haircuts. Ah, the nostalgia! I can't understand why everyone thinks it was so great. For me, it was a time of feeling weird. We didn't live in the suburbs, we didn't have a car, and I didn't have a dad. I never understood why I didn't. My mom, like all of the other mothers, wouldn't talk about him.

To be fair, there *were* many good things in the 1950s. After the end of the Korean War, there was peace and prosperity. The music was terrific, ranging from the continuation of 1940s' ballads to the beginnings of Rock and

Roll. Our parents hated it, and thus made us love it more. There were a variety of styles to listen to, from crooners like Pat Boone, to early country/rock legend Buddy Holly, to Elvis Presley, Chuck Berry, and Jerry Lee Lewis, who completely broke the mold. In those days, the records were forty-fives—for forty-five revolutions per minute—and if you were a lucky kid, you had a record player that those forty-fives fit on. Otherwise, you used a little plastic gadget that converted your thirty-three spindle to one that would hold a forty-five record.

I had the little plastic gadget. I can remember my mom buying me some records when I was young. One was "The Naughty Lady of Shady Lane," a cute little ditty recorded by The Ames Brothers in 1954, when I was eight. After listening to somewhat suggestive lyrics, you find out in the last line that it's about a baby. I still remember some of the words. Another memorable song for me was "Love Me Tender," one of Elvis's early hits, released in 1956. I was never a big Elvis fan, but I really liked that song. I think my mom regretted buying it, since I played it over and over and over. As you might imagine, I know all of those lyrics too.

The songs the record companies decided would be hits were always on the "A" side of the records. They were the ones that got the most airtime. Radio was the primary method for disseminating music in those days. What the artists or record companies considered leftovers went on the "B" or flip side of the record. Some of those B-side soundtracks weren't bad. In fact, Pat Boone's "April Love" and Elvis Presley's "Hound Dog" were on the B-side and both made the Billboard top 100. "Hound Dog" went to #1, but then again, it was Elvis—the "King of Rock and Roll."

I always loved music. I think that was a result of a combination of an early exposure to all kinds of compositions, from classical to top forty hits, and a genetic component. My mom and her brothers all played ukuleles and were constantly putting on "performances" in our living room. It was fun when I was a little kid, but horribly embarrassing when I became a sophisticated teenager.

Of course, living in Philadelphia, all that exposure to music and loving to dance led directly to *American Bandstand*. When I was fourteen, in 10th grade, my friend, Betty Ann and I went to the show several times. Somehow, her dad was able to get tickets for us, which were scarce as the proverbial hens' teeth. The studio where the show aired was small, holding about 200 jitterbugging teenagers. We rode the trolley to Market Street and then transferred to the El. We got off at 46th street, after the train became elevated (thus the name). We were instantly engulfed in a crowd of teenyboppers who couldn't wait to get in to see Dick Clark (mmm, dreamy) and whoever his featured act of the day was. That was great, but mostly, we wanted to dance.

In those days, girls could dance with girls, and it was no big deal, since they outnumbered the boys by a wide margin. While we never became any of the Bandstand regulars, it gave me a fun story to tell to non-Philadelphians over the years. They were always impressed. In fact, I suspect it was part of the reason David married me. Like many other teenaged boys, he was a big fan of Frannie Giordano, one of the regulars on the show. She was cute, had great blond hair, and could dance well. Needless to say, she was a popular girl.

David asked me, "Do you know Frannie Giordano?"

He was quite disappointed when I told him, "No, but I saw her every time I went."

Apparently, that was good enough, and the idea that he knew someone who went to Bandstand was sufficient to make me famous in his eyes. Even if I wasn't Frannie Giordano.

Some other good things in the fifties were the many technological breakthroughs that affected our lives, like televisions that were affordable. Although, many could argue how good that's been. In medicine, Jonas Salk's discovery of a vaccine for polio was a major breakthrough. Watson and Crick elucidating the structure of DNA in 1953 led to genetic testing, which is now becoming common-place. The Interstate Highway system was initiated, paving the way (pun intended) for Americans to travel more in their new Fords and Chevys. The Civil Rights movement got its start in the fifties when Rosa Parks refused to give up her seat and move to the back of the bus where the people of Alabama thought she belonged. There was even the beginning of the Space Race, with Sputnik's launch in 1957, which spurred America's entry into space-related technology and the founding of NASA. After all, we couldn't let those "Commie Russkies," as they were refer-red to back then, beat us to the moon.

As a kid, I remember those developments well. I vividly recall going to our doctor's office for those polio vacci-nations. There were three shots. I can remember being scared on the first visit. I didn't know what to expect, or if it would hurt, but, polio was a truly frightening disease. All of us who grew up then saw pictures of kids in iron lungs. We did not mind being stuck in the arm with polio vaccine—even if we were scared. I know I didn't, and neither did our mothers. In those days, unlike today's anti-vaxxer parents, everyone thought vaccines were wonderful things that spared us from dreadful diseases. Truth be told, they were, and still are.

Of course, had DNA not been discovered when it was, and so successfully developed since, I likely would never have had as many of my own revelations and found my family. I can remember as a child being excited about it, thinking how wonderful it would be to know about your own genetic makeup. Little did I know what a pivotal role it would play in my life. Now I do. The DNA testing we had done by 23andMe not only told us if we were related to anyone else in their database, but also gave us information on potential genetic disorders. Knowledge of some of those disorders can be lifesaving, like sensitivity to anti-coagulants, which I have. You can bet that any time I have to have surgery, I will be sure to let the doctors know about that. It also helped me find Rodney and Jacob.

The space race was another thing that excited me. I remember going outside at night to watch for Sputnik. I sky-gazed for days on end, watching a little bright dot moving across the sky and knowing that people had put that up there. I couldn't wait for the US to do something similar. Years later, I did the same thing when the International Space Station went into orbit. There's even an app now for your smart phone that helps you find the ISS's position in the sky. My, how far we've come. I always loved science, and I wanted to do something with the space program. However, that was before the days of ordinary people participating, not just test pilots.

Forty some-odd years later, in the waning days of the 1990s, and after several career changes, I got to work on a NASA-funded program on ground-penetrating laser radar called LiDAR (which stands for Light Detection and Ranging) One of my market research clients, who worked for a global oil and gas company, asked me to be part of their team to investigate the commercial feasibility of using LiDAR to detect ground subsidence. For those of you who aren't geologists or haven't been "in the oil patch," this simply means that the ground becomes compacted and is lower than it was at a previous time. Dictionary.com defines it as "the gradual sinking of landforms to a lower level as a result of earth movements, mining operations, etc." The sinkholes we're getting used to seeing are a type of subsidence.

Working on this project was an experience of a lifetime. We surveyed geeks who worked in large and small oil and gas companies, as well as academics who study ground movements. Our interviews gathered data that allowed us to determine whether LiDAR could be commercially successful. Along the way, I learned a lot about various types of satellites, and the importance of ground subsidence. Oil and gas companies are very interested in it, since it could lead to legal action for them if their withdrawal of oil or gas causes this land sinking and property damage. There was an entire upscale subdivision in Baytown, Texas that was lost to ground subsidence from water withdrawal from aquifers beneath it. Land near it sank an astonishing nine feet over a thirty-year period. That subdivision is now a nature preserve. Knowing about subsidence is critical for low-lying coastal areas, like Galveston and some areas of Houston, which are already prone to flooding from storm surges. I thought about that a lot when Hurricane Katrina hit New Orleans and Hurricane Ike hit the Texas coast.

Although we didn't find a huge amount of interest in the technology (there are other ways to measure subsidence), I gained insights into the technologies that are spin-offs from the space program, which are amazing, and far more numerous than most people realize. We presented our findings at Stennis Space Center in Mississippi and got to rub elbows with NASA personnel and an audience of geologists. Pretty cool stuff for a girl from South Philly.

Nevertheless, bad things happened in the fifties, too. It wasn't a decade filled with mothers who made apple pie and dressed to perfection, as many remember it.

Even after the service of all the women during World War II, like my mom, or those who held down men's jobs while the men were at war, there were near-universal "little woman" attitudes towards females. They were supposed to be perfectly dressed and have perfect hairdos, a perfect home, and perfect children. They were generally not allowed to wear pants unless they were riding a horse or doing some other "masculine" thing. And they certainly did not work. Those poor souls who had to work made even less money than men in a similar job—worse than it is today. In reading a biography of Ruth Bader Ginsberg, I've learned just how bad it was to be a woman who wanted to pursue a legal career in the 1950s. Even if you could get into law school—there were strict limits on how many females were admitted—trying to find a job other than a paralegal at that time was nearly impossible.

In addition, if you didn't fit the mold of the "perfect" family and live in the suburbs, you were a second-class citizen. Although I was too young to be aware of this, I'm sure my own mother fit into this category. While many women did lose their husbands in the war, neighbors and friends knew those stories well. Many even knew the soldier, who might have been a high-school sweetheart. But why was a single woman living with her parents and raising a child without a husband and no story to explain it? It was strange; that's what people thought. My mom and I just popped in out of the blue. Literally. We flew into Philadelphia on a transcontinental flight from LA, on which a nice Air Force pilot held me so my mom could get some lunch. I can remember being bullied as a kid by a particularly nasty girl who loved to taunt me, calling me a "weirdo without a father."

The J. Edgar Hoover and the McCarthy hearings stained that period in our history and ruined lives. It branded government employees, those in the entertainment industry, educators, and union activists as traitors for life, whether they were or not. It was a time of reckless, unsubstantiated accusations without proper regard for evidence or due process. In their zeal to eliminate the scourge of communism, Hoover et al. accused people of disloyalty, subversion, or treason. Fortunately, none of my family was directly touched by that, but the fear it engendered permeated the entire country. Because we were big consumers of TV news, I can vividly remember seeing people at those hearings with near-panicked looks on their faces. It was only as I got older that I understood why.

Television had a huge impact on those of us growing up during the fifties. My family got our first TV in 1952, when I was six years old. It was a black & white RCA, a huge box that was five times the size of its twelve-inch screen. I had to sit up close to actually see the screen, sitting cross-legged on our mail-order Olson rug. The TV didn't have a remote; I had to get up off the sofa or the floor to change the channels. Inside the cabinet were many mysterious tubes that glowed when it was turned on. The technology was really cool to me then.

In those days, TV programs consisted of game shows, local programs, and sitcoms produced by the "big three" networks of ABC, CBS, and NBC. It was also the beginning of the televised soap operas, daytime dramas that were supported by advertising from "soap" companies like Proctor & Gamble, who packaged things like dishtowels in their soap boxes to encourage purchases. I didn't care about them, and neither did my mom or grandmother. I watched local shows like *Flash Gordon*, who constantly battled *Ming the Merciless*. There was also *Willie the Worm*, *Chief Halftown*, and *Bertie the Bunyip*. Those last three were probably more acceptable fare for a six-year old, but I loved Flash Gordon.

Bertie the Bunyip—a mythical Australian creature who was a cross between a bunny, a collie dog, and a duck-billed platypus. Fair use from Wikipedia.

There were daytime game shows that my Mom and my grandmother and I watched. They were broadcast on the local stations. When you knew the answers to the questions they posed, you just called in—as quickly as you could. And that wasn't easy with a rotary dial phone. If you were lucky enough to be the first caller, and you knew the correct answers, you'd win prizes. I loved watching them try to answer the questions posed. The most exciting time was a show that asked who the Chief Justice of the Supreme Court was. My mom and grandmother both knew, and my mom hit the phone hard and fast. She was the first caller and won some nifty stuff by knowing his name was Earl Warren. Although neither of these women had any formal education beyond high school, they both read like fiends, and followed the national and local news religiously. I may not know all the Supreme Court justices, but I distinctly remember Earl Warren. I still have the Oneida silver service and the set of glasses from that loot and think about my mom and grandmother every time we use them.

The network sitcoms like *Father Knows Best*, *Ozzie & Harriet*, and *Leave it to Beaver* portrayed model families composed of a father, a mother, and two kids. Those idyllic families sat on their new sofas in their new clothes watching their new TVs in their new suburban homes. I didn't have anything even close to that. Neither did any of my unknown-at-the-time siblings. We were the weird ones.

Chapter Twenty-Four

The Kids' Lives

"Being an only child is a disease in itself."
G. STANLEY HALL

The 1950s were not a dream come true for everyone. Carolyn, Ted, Liz, Eddie, and I grew up in single-parent households, or with step-parents, which were decidedly not the norm back then. Single-parent families lived with the stigma of being different, odd, not complete. Many of those women were excluded from gatherings that included husbands, or even ladies' lunches. All of the children born of the relationships between Clarence and the mothers—Ethel (Carolyn's mom), Maria (Ted's mom), Irene (my mom), and Angelina (Liz and Eddie's mom)— who ended up in single-parent homes, shared that we struggled our whole lives to understand who we were and why we weren't in the "perfect" families that we saw on TV. We thought that's how things were supposed to be.

It's possible that we might have been helped by understanding better why our mothers did—or did not—do what they did. Knowing and understanding more about our common father beyond some grainy old black and white photographs might have helped—it did to an extent for Liz and Eddie. That wasn't the case for Carolyn, Ted, and me. We were left to fill things in with our own imaginations. Like most children, our imaginations ran wild in a bad way.

Rodney's situation was different. After spending his first four years in an orphanage, two loving, adoptive parents found him, so he lived a more "normal" childhood. Until we found each other (thank you, *23andMe*), he and his son wondered who his birth parents were and how he came to be adopted. Unless he decides to get his adoption records unsealed, we won't know all of the details of that. At least he now knows who his birth father was. And he knows he has at least five half-brothers and sisters.

I had a good early childhood, with an adoring mother and two equally adoring grandparents. Even my grandfather finally cut back on his drinking binges, but he didn't eliminate them completely. I can remember as a child walking up the street to that tap room to fetch him and bring him home for dinner, just as my mother had.

Like Carolyn, my grandmother, who I called Nana, spent a lot of time with me. Although bed-ridden, she could still balance a little girl on her lap. She sang me funny songs like "Tough Guy Levi is My Name and I'm a Yiddish Cowboy." She told me family stories, like the one about her great-grandfather, who was a shoemaker, and who also invented a speed indicator for machinery. She loved to tell how she and her sister came to marry two brothers. I also had two uncles, two aunts, two cousins, and a host of second and third cousins. They all came to visit my grandmother, the matriarch of the family. In those days, when people came over to your house to visit, it was called "having company." We had company a lot, and I loved it.

A very young author and her Nana. Personal photo.

That was my world. It was great as a little girl, but as I grew up, I began to wonder why I didn't have a father like my friends did. My mother told me he was killed in the war; her eyes and her body language told me otherwise. I never believed her. Although children are not as savvy as grownups, they can sense when someone is evading the truth. My mother excelled at many things, but lying was not one of them. I can remember thinking for years that there must have been more. Now I know there was—a lot more. Although my half-siblings and I have been able to piece much of the stories together, we also realize there are some things we'll never know.

Like Carolyn and Ted, I watched 1950s family sitcoms like *Leave it to Beaver* and *Ozzie & Harriet*. We've shared how we believed we were different—weird. And, just as all kids do, we blamed ourselves. I remember being convinced that it was my fault, and always felt that something was wrong with me. Carolyn and Ted told me the same thing. I constantly asked my mother about my father. Just like Ethel and Maria, my mom would never talk about him. Eventually, like Carolyn and Ted, I stopped asking. Liz and

Eddie heard a bit more, since their mother, Angelina, never said anything bad about him, just that they couldn't make their marriage work.

For years, I was convinced that I must have been adopted, or came from a horrible family situation. Maybe one of my parents murdered the other? Or, worse yet, maybe my "real" parents didn't want me, and that's why they gave me up for adoption. There must have been something about me that was not "right." Otherwise, why would they give me up? I never believed that I looked anything like my mother, who I thought was beautiful. She had gorgeous naturally wavy, shiny, brunette hair, unlike my curly, frizzy mop. She had beautiful fingernails. I had things on my fingertips approaching the consistency of tissue paper that constantly tore. So, I did the best thing that I could think to do. I bit them off so they couldn't tear. And then I got into trouble for doing that.

Many of my friends had two parents. Why didn't I? Why did my mother and I live with her parents? My two uncles had spouses, and one had two children. Why did they have "normal" lives, and I didn't? They had cars. We never did. One thing that would work in my favor later on is I was smart, so I made terrific grades in school. Yet, this was just one more thing that made me different. I was unquestionably weird. And in those days before geeks and nerds were fashionable, weird was painful. I grew up with too many questions, and no answers. This was not because my mother was quiet. In fact, she was very outgoing, and we talked about a lot of things. But, my father was not one of them.

Carolyn, Ted, and I shared that they'd felt the same awkwardness as children as I had. They'd had similar feelings. We had all felt strange—different. I realize that most kids may think they're weird, but it was accentuated for us by having only one parent. In addition, that parent wouldn't talk. None of us ever knew much, or anything, about our Dad. Ted met him twice for brief meetings in Hawaii, but he was older then, and never got to know him well. Even Liz and Eddie, as sister and brother, felt this way to some extent, and they knew him better than the rest of us. In addition, they only spent a small portion of their lives with him. Rodney, by contrast, had two adoptive parents, so he didn't agonize over this the way the rest of us did.

Our mothers, to some degree or another, lived their lives through their children. They were determined to make a better life for each of us than the life they'd experienced. We'd finish high school, go to college, and make something of ourselves. They were single-minded in their desire to see us do better than they did. Fortunately, all of us inherited some intelligence genes, so we did well in school, and three of us went on to finish at least some college.

Being in that situation puts a heavy burden on a kid—it's not easy to feel like you're living someone else's life for them. My mom always pushed me to study hard and do well in school. She did what she could to help me when I got stuck on something and inserted herself even at times when she wasn't needed. She always provided many outside school activities to enrich my life. We became thoroughly knowledgeable about every museum in Philadelphia. She was thrilled when I got into orchestra and drama in junior high and a capella choir in high school. My orchestra career turned out to be very short. I have always loved music, but they gave me a flute when I wanted a clarinet. So, being stubborn and wanting to get my way, I quit. Now, after hearing James Galway perform, I wish I'd stuck with that flute.

Having my mom constantly tell me that she didn't want me to end up like her and not finish high school, put a tremendous amount of pressure on me. This made me feel that I always had to do and say the right things. You're not living your life for one, but for two people. And one of those people is your mother, whom you wouldn't want to disappoint for anything in the world.

Four of us—Carolyn, Ted, Rodney, and I—were only children. This was another thing that made us weird. Many of our friends had brothers or sisters, or sometimes both. Liz and Eddie had each other, but big sisters tend to ignore their little brothers, and Liz did until many years later. Interestingly, my closest friends were also singles. Maybe misery loves company? And many of my friends were "the smart kids," too. The weirdoes clumped together, just as they always have and always will.

Anita, my best friend through junior high and high school, had two parents. I was always envious of that. Years later, after I had found my siblings, I learned that her childhood was not the perfect one I imagined it to be and was probably worse than mine. She told me that she'd had an abusive father and a passive-aggressive mother. Fortunately, like Carolyn and me, she had a terrific grandmother who lived nearby. She was her refuge.

I was jealous of my cousins because they had each other, a nice house, a car, and better clothes than I ever had (which became embarrassing hand-me-downs for me). While I was writing this memoir, my cousin, Mary Lou told me that when their mother passed away, she and her brother were split up between two of her mother's sisters and their families. So much for the ideal childhood.

But the grass is always greener—especially when you're a kid.

We Latham kids also struggled with relationships. The three of us who'd had no or next to no time with our dad never had a consistent male presence in our lives, so we did not see firsthand what a "normal" husband-wife relationship should look like. Our role models were on TV and seeing those sitcoms like *Leave it to Beaver* and *Father Knows Best* only made us wish for more in our lives. True, I had my grandparents, but they were old. My grand-mother was ill and bedridden, so in my mind their relationship didn't count as a real marriage. As a result, we all had difficulties of one sort or another with the opposite sex.

For instance, I was always attracted to older men. I dated two guys who were significantly older than I was when I was in high school. People might even consider that illegal today. One of them was a friend of one of my numerous second or third cousins. He was twenty-six when he took me to my senior prom. I was seventeen. He was a nice guy and never pushed me to do anything nice girls shouldn't have done. If he had, the cousins who'd introduced us probably would have killed him. I eventually realized that he was just too old for me and ended it.

The other man was in the Navy and I met him through church, where he visited to sing in the choir. He had a fine baritone voice, was nice to look at, and he was an officer. And, yes, a gentleman. This was pretty impressive stuff for a high-schooler! Although she never said a word, I am sure that my mother was horrified with the relationship. In hindsight, I am amazed that she let it happen at all. Bruce was from Seattle, Washington, where his parents owned a hotel. He traveled a lot in his Navy career, and we wrote to each other for several years.

He sent me Ma Griffe perfume from Paris. *Sigh.* It was real perfume, too, not cologne. It's still available and is described as a Chypre floral fragrance, the most sophisticated and beautiful of fragrance families. It's floral, with woody, mossy accents. Chypre is thought to be named after Cypress, the island birthplace of Aphrodite, the goddess of love. *Sigh again.* I loved it and used it all up.

I realize now that in those older guys, I was looking for a daddy figure.

Only one of us didn't go through multiple marriages. I was the exception. I married my college sweetheart, and we've been together for a half century. I think there are many reasons for that; I suspect that the biggest one is that we've always been friends, and fellow geeks. Thankfully, David couldn't be more different than I now know my dad was, or we wouldn't still be married. Unlike many women, I did not marry someone just like my dad. Since I never knew him, how could I?

Insecurities plagued me growing up and remained with me for most of my life. I learned to hide it well. I learned discipline and "stick-to-itiveness" from my Marine Corps Featherneck mom. Both of those traits got me through a lot of things. My mom always told me that I could be whatever I wanted to be, and that she'd be there to back me up. She worked diligently on me when I was in high school, constantly checking to be sure I was doing my homework and encouraged me to read as much as possible. She was involved in parent teacher organizations. My best friend, Anita, stayed on me, too. My idea of a great career at the time was to be an X-ray technician.

When she heard about that, Anita said, "Bullshit. You're going to college!"

My mom loved her for that. She had never finished high school because of the Depression. No one in my family had ever gone to college. She was determined that her child was going to be the first.

When it came time for me to consider where I might go and how we'd pay for it, my mom swung into action. She worked her fingers off identifying potential scholarships. Not so easy in the pre-Google days. She found one that was run by two influential Philadelphians: Reverend William H. Gray, Jr., then pastor of the Bright Hope Baptist Church in North Philadelphia; and Milton Shapp, an early cable TV pioneer who subsequently became governor of Pennsylvania. I applied, wrote an essay, and made it through the initial screening process. The next step was an interview with Reverend Gray and Mr. Shapp. It was my first encounter with "important" people, and I was extremely nervous.

I had decided at this point that I wanted to study microbiology, so I could learn more about bacteriophages; little viral creatures that eat bacteria. I learned about them in high school biology and was convinced they could cure diseases like the common cold. I knew that I wanted to go to a small college—Philadelphia College of Pharmacy and Science (PCP&S), now called University of the Sciences in Philadelphia. Reverend Gray and Mr. Shapp, for their part, thought I should go to Temple University. The tuition there was lower, so the scholarship money would go further, and they had ties with the administration who would keep a close eye on their scholarship students.

In the interview, my challenge was to prove to them why going to PCP & S was a better choice for me. I managed to overcome my nervousness and presented them with arguments of smaller class sizes and a stronger emphasis on science. I won them over. I entered the following fall, earning the Shapp Scholarship, plus a scholarship from the school. That, combined with working part-time in the Dean's office, and some student loans, got me through. Not bad for an insecure kid. Although I found that interview nerve-wracking, I managed to stay calm and logical. That won the day for me.

Although I started in college as a microbiology major, a summer's work experience at a VA Hospital in the Radio-chemistry Lab convinced me to change my course of study. That, and the fact that the microbiology lab in the hospital smelled really bad.

My Marine Corps mom was chest-thumping proud that I won that scholarship. I was beginning to learn how to fake it. If you look and sound like you know what you're talking about, you can usually get your way. Recently, Amy Cuddy, a researcher at Harvard University who studies body language and the impact it has on your hormones, has classified a number of body poses that can actually increase your testosterone (power hormone) and reduce your cortisol levels (stress hormone) to help you boost your confidence. It's easy. You just strike a "power pose"—like Wonder Woman—for two minutes a day. I'm not making this up, Cuddy has data to prove it.

Part of my mom's drive came from her desire to prove that even though she'd had a child out of wedlock, that child could become a "somebody."

I can remember as a teenager overhearing her being berated by her brother, Sam, when he told her, "Rene, if you hadn't fooled around with that sailor, you wouldn't be in the mess you're in now."

She retorted, "My life is not a mess. I'm perfectly happy and have a wonderful little girl who will make something of herself one day. Besides that, without me, who would take care of our mother? I know for sure that you and our brother Frank wouldn't do it."

Kids may not know everything, but they can sense when someone doesn't think well of them. Until he got much older, I never felt accepted by Uncle Sam. By contrast, my Uncle Frank always accepted me, and loved me unconditionally until the day he died. My mom's relationship with Aunt Carrie ("Doc" Rosenbach's mistress of forty years) was likely thrown in her face, too. The fifties were not a time of acceptance for women who didn't fit the established mold. And my mom, the Featherneck, never did.

Chapter Twenty-Five

Sibling Relationships

"Certainly, people can get along without siblings. Single children do, and there are people who have irreparably estranged relationships with their siblings who live full and satisfying lives, but to have siblings and not make the most of that resource is squandering one of the greatest interpersonal resources you'll ever have."
JEFFREY KLUGER

By 2008, four of the then-known five of us had established contact and we began to stay in touch with each other on a regular basis. Carolyn and I communicated by phone and she sent me cards on birthdays and holidays. Liz and I talked incessantly by phone and became very close. Ted and I texted and talked by phone. We all still stay in touch one way or another. None of us puts demands on the others. When we're ready to talk, we talk.

Meanwhile, Liz and her husband Ron met up with Carolyn on a trip near her home. Her husband, Mike, never came along. We suspect that was a clue, that Mike may not have been as pleased about this new family as the rest of us were. Although sadly, since he passed away, Carolyn has been more open and communicative with us. We think it was just something he was not comfortable with. We understand it's not something everyone could accept.

A couple of years later, I did some focus groups for a client on industrial lubricants used in trucks or farming equipment. We started in Roanoke, Virginia, and Haddonfield, New Jersey. My client contact for the project and I thought that we should also get some input from the West coast, and that a city in California, smaller than LA or San Francisco, nearer to agricultural areas, would be a good place. I decided that Sacramento would be ideal, and my client agreed. She knew the broad outline of my discoveries and was more than happy to help me spend more time with one of my newfound sisters. I finished up my groups, bid goodbye to my client, and met up with Liz and her husband. We spent a couple of great days together. We shared meals, with wine, of course, visited a winery, did a couple of shopping trips, and bonded even more.

Ted and his wife travel to California regularly and frequently visit with his daughter, so he sees Liz and her husband more often than the rest of us. Liz sees Ted's daughter, meeting for an occasional lunch or a glass of wine. They live less than 20 miles away from each other and never knew about their relationship, or how close they were geographically, until we made our discoveries.

Jacob, Rodney's son, who led to Rodney's discovery through 23andMe, met Liz on a trip from Hawaii to California, so the sixth child and his son are coming into the fold.

One of the things we decided in those early years was that it was probably a good thing we didn't meet up sooner. By the time all of our revelations occurred, we were older, more mellow, and probably far less judgmental than we likely were in our younger years. We'd matured enough by that time to realize there were no hard and fast right or wrong rules to live your life, and that all of our moms and our dad were products of their environments. Their thoughts, emotions, actions, and behaviors were tied to how they experienced the world and how the world shaped them, just as ours were. They were all young, and living in a difficult, wartime setting when people didn't know from one day to the next whether they'd ever see each other again, or even be alive. Who were we to judge them and their actions?

As we connected, we wondered why our mothers wouldn't talk about our dad. We wanted to understand what drove them to do what they did. We think part of it was the issue of being a single parent, which was not as easily accepted then as it is now. Some of it was probably that our dad was a typical sailor, with a girl in every port. Likely more than one. Much of it was that people didn't share their family "issues" then as they do now. I realized that fact after learning about my best friend's dysfunctional family, with an abusive father and a passive/aggressive mother, and about how my cousins were split up after their Mom died. I never knew about either of those things when I was growing up. Maybe if I had, it would have helped me. At least I would have known I wasn't the only one without an ideal family.

After years of wondering why my mom never dated or had any romantic relationships, writing this book has given me some clues as to why she didn't. An alcoholic father who chased off potential suitors began the trend of deciding that men were not that important in her life. Carl, the married Marine, was the next disappointment. Clarence the Charming was the last disillusionment. Finally, having a brother who looked down his nose at her and struggled to accept her child likely clinched it for her. When something awful happens, it's not something to talk about easily. Especially to a child. She never wanted to talk to me about it as an adult either.

After David and I were married, and my grandparents had passed away, she was now a "free" woman who could pursue her own life. I asked her, "Why don't you start dating?"

Her response was, "I just don't think that's an important part of my life. And I never had much luck with men."

When comparing notes on our mothers, we found that our dad tried to reconnect with four of the six of us. After their mothers passed away, Carolyn, Liz, and Ted all found letters he'd written to their mothers. There was no evidence that they'd ever answered those letters. I found nothing like that. Combined with the misspelling of his name on my birth certificate, I strongly suspect that our dad never knew anything more about me than that my mom was pregnant. Maybe he didn't even know that. Although we can't know this for sure, I suspect he never knew about Rodney either.

After we all connected, Liz discovered that our dad married a third time. After he and her mom divorced, he moved to Montana and met a woman who owned a restaurant and bar. In one of life's little ironies, our recovering alcoholic father took over the bartender duties, and they eventually married. She had three sons by a previous marriage, and of any of his children, they got to know him the best. By this time, he'd finally gotten his life together, and they told Liz and me what a great guy he was. Aside from his health, at least he had a somewhat happy ending.

We now have a better understanding of our dad and our moms. We've shared our stories and theirs and pieced together what little we know. But those women who were such a big part of Clarence's life and ours remained silent their whole lives and took what they knew to their graves.

Chapter Twenty-Six

Family Before, Family After

"Feelings of worth can flourish only in an atmosphere where individual differences are appreciated, mistakes are tolerated, communication is open, and rules are flexible—the kind of atmosphere that is found in a nurturing family."
VIRGINIA SATIR

Even before all of my searching and discoveries, I had what most people would consider a fine adult life. David and I both had good jobs and made decent salaries. Although not rich, we were financially comfortable. I was accepted as a member of his big family. I always felt I fit in with them and was loved by them as much as they loved David. We were especially close to one of his sisters, Jean, who still lived in the same little town in Pennsylvania where he grew up. We spent most trips in Vintondale at Jean's house. I vividly remember going there for the first time, before we were married or had a car. We journeyed on a Greyhound bus—an adventure in itself, and a beautiful trip.

The route took us through many, many towns. We first went non-stop from Philadelphia to Harrisburg, where we changed buses. It then went on to smaller towns like Mifflintown, Lewisburg, State College (home of Penn

State), Hollidaysburg, and Ebensburg. Our final stop was in Mundy's Corner, eight hilly miles from David's home of Vintondale. Jean's husband, Johnny, picked us up for the final leg of our journey. Going on the bus was fine, despite all the stops, and gave me a chance to see parts of Pennsylvania I'd never been to. Coming back to Philadelphia was another story. While in Vintondale, I drank a glass of the wonderful water David had bragged about for so many years. The bus returning had no restroom, so you can probably guess how well I tolerated that water. But it did taste good. Fortunately, that bus back to Philadelphia made many stops along the way, and I took advantage of them all.

One of David's brothers, Clyde, was more like a father to him. He had served in the infantry in Europe in WWII and came home with what is now referred to as PTSD. He never married. He coached David as my mom had taught me, encouraging him to study hard, and get good grades so he could go to college and not have to work in the coal mines.

Without Clyde and his financing, David likely would have never gone to college and met me. When he heard we were coming back, he thought it might be funny to test this city girl David was bringing home.

We were standing outside Jean's house, talking about big cities and small towns, when Clyde said, "Wait a minute. I have something for you."

He came back with a big, brown bag that looked pretty heavy. I have always loved surprises, so I opened that bag quickly. Inside was a gorgeous, huge Black Rat Snake. What Clyde didn't know was that that I was not the least bit afraid of snakes and knew that this was not a venomous one.

I squealed, "Ooooh, he's beautiful!"

The crestfallen look on Clyde's face was priceless, but it helped him to decide that I was probably okay.

One of Jean's daughters, Leslie, who now has a daughter, a son, and grandchildren of her own, spent the entire time we were there following me around. Another daughter, Barb, took over as matriarch when Jean passed away, and we are still very close with her and her two sons and their families. Sandy, who took years to work up the nerve to learn to drive, is married to Roger, a great guy who's a whiz at remodeling and construction. Bob, the oldest, and his wife, Emily, stay in touch regularly. I not only had a good extended family then, but still do today.

We were not as close with David's other brothers and sisters, since they were spread out over a huge geographic area, from nearby east coast regions like New York, Connecticut, and Washington, DC, to a small town in Alberta, Canada. Nevertheless, when we were in those areas, we always tried to see them, and they occasionally came back to home base to visit. When we knew they'd be there, we made sure to be there, too.

David and I both grew up without a lot of money, he much more so than me. His family had times when they relied heavily on "government cheese," one of the things families on welfare or some other government relief got to help them survive. Neither his dad nor his mother worked, and they did whatever they had to do to get by. His dad was disabled and got about fifty dollars a month in Social Security. They hated taking handouts, but at least they didn't starve. To this day, David still balks about accepting anything that even remotely feels like charity to him. In addition to that government cheese, his family ate a lot of bread and potatoes, plus whatever else was cheap and would fill an empty tummy.

By contrast, I felt bad because I got hand-me-down clothes and couldn't go shopping as much as some of my friends did, or get my hair done—unless we were going to have school graduation pictures taken. David still tells me that I was a spoiled rich kid when I was growing up. The reality is that my mother and my grandparents and I survived on a City of Philadelphia pension and Social Security.

After starting his working life as a printer, my grandfather got a steady job with good benefits as a Deputy Real Estate Assessor in Philadelphia and stayed there until retirement. Much of our ability to make it was thanks to a grandmother and a mother who were exceptional money managers. They kept track of every penny that came into and went out of our home. In addition to the recurring outlays shown in the image of one month of their ledgers, there were monthly amounts for groceries, regular charitable contributions, and occasional expenses for home repairs and furnishings. Frequently, amounts were also put into the bank for saving. We weren't rich, but compared to what David's family had, it certainly might have seemed that way.

In looking through that book from 1951, I made several discoveries. My grandmother had rheumatoid arthritis, which crippled her hands to the point where they were nearly useless. Nevertheless, somehow, she managed to write, and she could even hold a paintbrush. She was meticulous about documenting everything financial. My mother was the same way, and David and I are too. Except ours is electronic, in Quicken.

Nana took that ability to hold a paintbrush to create paint-by-number artwork. She not only stayed within the lines, but she also improved those paintings significantly by adding shading and lightening dark areas. We had

One month of my family's ledger. I was six years
old at this time. David and I used to keep a ledger
too before computers. It's interesting to see
how prices have changed. Personal photo.

them all over the house. I still have one of a woman who reminds me of my mom. Our grandchildren swear to this day that her eyes follow them, so when they were younger I had to take that portrait off the wall in the bedroom where they stayed. I told them it was my mom keeping watch on them to be sure they were safe, but it totally spooked them. In the back of that journal is a listing of the paintings my Nana produced. Although many of them were given away, she sold some, to the tune of $200 each. That was a lot of money at that time, compared to the $250 in social security and pension money they took in monthly. I never knew that until I read that journal more carefully.

David and I didn't have much money when we were first married. He was and still is a maniac about saving, so we did whatever we could to stay within our means. Generally, we did a pretty good job of it. Unlike many of our friends, I wasn't a big spender. We never had the big houses and new cars that many of them had. Aside from student loans, we weren't in a lot of debt either. It did make us feel bad, though. We always worried about why we weren't "doing better." And it fed my insecurities about myself. I still wasn't as good as other people.

Unlike some of my friends and family, I have a terrific spouse and a great son. We have two grandchildren who keep us young. I've had an interesting career and have met many remarkable people, some of whom have become good friends. We've lived in various places in the United States, and I had opportunities for business travel outside the US. Fortunately, as our finances improved over the years, we were able to take voyages in ways other than on a Greyhound bus. Although we started out on shaky economic ground, with a baby who was a surprise, plus college and grad school loans to pay off, we're now fiscally comfortable. Even in retirement, thanks to David's nearly obsessive savings habits, we have a nice home, filled with too much stuff we don't need. We live in a great area and are now close to our son and his family. In addition, there are terrific restaurants we can go to when we don't feel like cooking.

Nevertheless, even with all that, there was always a little nagging voice inside me that said I was not as good as everyone else. For example, Anita, my best friend from school who nagged me into going to college, was married to her high school sweetheart and lived in a beautiful home in a perfect suburban neighborhood. They had it all. The American Dream. A large home filled with lots of the stuff that society tells us we need, and two cars in their attached garage. They both worked, and they made more money than David and I did in the medical research field. Proving that money wasn't everything in a relationship, he ultimately cheated on her. She divorced him, and that was the end of Anita's American Dream. She was smart, so hired a bulldog divorce lawyer, and came out of it financially strong, keeping the house and all of its contents.

David and I, meanwhile, soldiered on in our little apartment, with lower salaries, a baby, and college loan debts. We also had David's brother living with us, to save him from the perils of Western Pennsylvania, where he likely would have become a high-school dropout, working in the coal mines—if he'd been able to find any work at all. We got him back into school, and he's had a good life away from those coal mines. Although we didn't have the big houses and new cars, we had something better. A family with values that were in the right place, high standards, and love for one another.

I had to work extra hard to meet up to my own, probably unrealistic, expectations. That caused me a lot of angst during my career, and it likely held me back from accomplishing all I could have. I had a bad habit of trying too hard. It made other people who didn't work as intensely as I did look bad. It affected me when I was in large companies, where not being one of the "cool kids" hurt as much as it did in high school. I wasn't a cool kid there either, even among my circle of nerdy friends. I was in a group called CBB—College Bound Block—and we took special classes that the cool kids (who weren't as smart as we were) didn't qualify for. Fortunately, I was and still am highly competitive. I have the drive, but my execution was not always as flawless as it could have been.

During my career, I can vividly remember several occasions where I lost my cool when my superiors suggested doing something I thought was stupid. Although not in as many words, I would often tell them so. This was obviously not a good way to win over the people in the company who could have helped my career. I was certainly no diplomat. I suspect my mom, the Featherneck, found herself in these situations too. Fortunately, I think I've finally gotten over that. I'm retired now, so I don't have to put up with those dumb people any more.

That competitiveness and drive got me out of a good, but dead-end job at a hospital clinical lab, and into a graduate program at The Wharton School, part of the University of Pennsylvania, one of the top business schools in the world. Thanks to that lab job, I had a bit of a leg up, since the hospital was part of the university. That meant I could take courses without paying tuition, so the only outlay was for fees and books.

I knew I wanted to do something else, but didn't know what. Out of a world of possible career options, I only knew of one—science, specifically chemistry, in which I have a Bachelor's degree. So much for high school guidance counseling. I began by exploring the options that Penn offered. Although I would have loved to study astronomy, I knew that a four-year program was out of the question. In addition, I wasn't sure I had the math skills I'd need. Eventually, I found my way to Wharton and met with the Dean of the evening school, which was part of the undergraduate program. He suggested I take an accounting course and a marketing course, to see if either appealed to me. While I aced the accounting, I found it boring, but loved the marketing. Our marketing professor, Scott Armstrong, who still teaches at Wharton, got to know me and liked my work.

After class one evening, we had a discussion about the work I'd been doing, and how pleased he was to see how quickly I caught on to the concepts of marketing.

I asked him, "What can a chemistry major do with the rest of her life?"

Without missing a beat, he told me, "You should apply to the graduate school and get an MBA."

Dummy that I was, I asked, "What's an MBA?"

Scott patiently explained it was a Master's in Business Administration, and that Wharton was always in search of smart people with technical undergraduate degrees for their MBA program.

He set my life on a new path and will always be one of my heroes.

When I enrolled at Wharton, our son was starting kindergarten, and I commuted from a northeastern suburb of Philadelphia to the Penn campus, 20 miles away. It was a struggle for me and especially for David, who took a second job to help us survive. Unfortunately, that free tuition didn't apply in graduate school, since I was no longer an employee of the university. David's second job and student loans helped pay for it. Our son, Mike, went happily through kindergarten and first grade during this time, and didn't seem to be affected by it at all.

Wharton was a tough two-year journey for a scared girl from South Philly with zero business experience. In spite of that, I managed to do it, and it set the stage for the rest of our lives. I really enjoyed the classes, learned a lot, and made many friends with whom I still stay in touch.

Despite the school touting "The Wharton Experience"—a series of learning and growing events that would prepare you to become a polished business executive—my most vivid memory is of having to take a computer programming class. As a newly admitted student, I was required, along with everyone else, to learn programming. In those days (1973) that meant Fortran, with all of its glorious if/then statements. There were three alternatives: a two-week course; a six-week course; or a half-year course in addition to the other courses I'd have to take in my first semester. Since I had programmed an Olivetti calculator at my dead-end lab job, I thought, *how hard could this be?* I opted for the two-week course. Bad, bad choice.

To do Fortran programming back in those days before Tandys or Macs meant I had to use punch cards, which I prepared at the school. That was followed by a trek over to the computer center on campus, which was six blocks away. In August, in extreme heat and humidity. Then I waited for a printout of the results of my valiant efforts. Most of them said ERROR multiple times. Needless to say, there were a lot of trips, and a lot of ERRORs. This was repeated ad nauseum, until I got it just right. Computers at that time were even stupider than they are today, and if you didn't give them exact instructions, in the exact sequence, they'd bomb. The ERRORs meant that you were expecting the computer to be smart and know what you were thinking. I used to go home, at midnight sometimes, and just cry from frustration and inadequacy.

David was my cheerleader, and he repeatedly told me, "You're not the only one having problems. Just keep at it. You'll get through this. You've been through a lot worse."

He was right. I got through Wharton with flying colors. I graduated and became a newly-minted Master of Business Administration (MBA). My mom was thrilled beyond words. Not only was her little girl a college graduate, but she also had gotten a Master's degree. I was the only one in my family to accomplish that. My mom, I know, boasted about it, likely to the dismay of anyone who was within earshot. That MBA took us from Philadelphia to a corporate gig in Toledo, Ohio, and eventually to Texas. It was very rewarding, both from a financial and a career standpoint. It also brought our son, Mike, to Texas, where he met his wife, Trish.

Before my family discoveries, I had ridiculous fears. I was scared witless of roaches. I know, silly for someone who had no fear of snakes. Trust me, this is not a good thing when you live in southeast Texas. Maybe it was a hangover from my Mom's tales of flying roaches at Camp Lejeune. I can remember coming to Houston on a business trip and seeing a BIG roach in my room.

I called David, who told me, "Just squash the damned thing."

I ended up chasing it out of the room. There were probably more where he came from, and I didn't sleep well that night.

Worse than roach fears, I was afraid of getting water on my face. I couldn't even put my face under the shower without panicking. Pretty ridiculous for someone who had done a lot of difficult things in her life, but phobias are not logical. That fear of water kept me from learning to swim, so anytime I was with people at the beach or at a pool, I was the weird one who didn't join in the fun.

Chapter Twenty-Seven

How Things Will Never Be the Same Again

"In the sweetness of friendship let there be laughter, and sharing of pleasures. For in the dew of little things the heart finds its morning and is refreshed."
KHALIL GIBRAN

After I found out that I was not a loner, my feelings about myself began to change. And, once I connected with my new-found siblings, those changes continued. I was not alone any more. I was not a weirdo with half a family. Well, I was, but I was not the only one who was put in that position by the charming Clarence.

In researching my dad's Naval history, and hearing what little my half-brothers and half-sisters knew about him, I got a better idea of the kind of person Clarence was. He was not stupid, but he was uneducated, so he likely had a fairly narrow view of the world. His love of girls and a good time seemed to be his defining characteristics, and he spent a great deal of time pursuing those skirts—as many as he could. He wasn't a good husband or partner to any of the women with whom he had children, and maybe should never have been married. It seems he tried to stay single until he married Angelina, Liz and Eddie's mom. At that point, he was older, and probably more mature. I'm sorry I never got to meet him, but glad in a way that I didn't, since I'm not sure he ever knew about me, and don't know how he would have reacted. I don't harbor any bad feelings toward him, and realize that if not for his womanizing habits, I wouldn't be here. However, I wish he'd treated my mom better. She certainly deserved it.

The empty spot that I'd held inside me for so long as an only child began to be filled with a realization that there was nothing wrong with me. No more so than it was with Carolyn, Ted, Liz, Eddie, or Rodney. Or anyone else for that matter. We kids had done nothing wrong. What our father and mothers did wasn't any of our doing. And, as we got to know each other better, we found that we were some terrific people. We all have wonderful senses of humor, and we've had good lives. My siblings and I enjoy great kids who are doing well, and grandchildren who seem to be on the right track. The family circle is closing at long last.

My silly fears are almost gone. I can kill roaches with the best of them. I can put my head under the shower. This was an amazing accomplishment for me. I started working with a dive instructor who persuaded me to try a snorkel. I took swimming lessons and water aerobics. Now, I can actually swim short distances without going into a total panic. I'm not completely there yet, but I think if I fell in the water, I probably wouldn't drown.

My client relationships improved. I became firmer about what could and could not be done. I stopped being a pushover and raised my hourly rates. My business bloomed.

If people had told me that this could happen, I would not have believed them. But it did. It continues to develop as my new family gets closer and we interact more.

Life is good.

And it gets better with every passing day. David and I are now retired, as are most of my siblings. This gives me time to write something more interesting than market research reports, and I'm learning to be a "real" writer. I've had a short story mystery published in an anthology and another short story published in an online literary magazine. I'm a published author. Now that we have more free time, we travel more. We've seen a lot of the world, and especially enjoy cruising—particularly on the smaller ships.

After all my searching and discoveries, I read on some medical websites that the hereditability of familial tremor is still in question. I even contacted a leading researcher in this disease in Los Angeles, and he told me the same thing. It is just not known with any certainty whether it is inherited or not. So far, none of my siblings have had any symptoms. Yet, having that disease led me on a path of discovery that literally changed my life. Thanks to that diagnosis, I began a search for a family medical history. Instead I found a family.

Together, we have broken the silence of our mothers.

"If you cannot get rid of the family skeleton, you may as well make it dance." George Bernard Shaw

Abbreviated Genealogy Information

The following page shows my genealogy only, on both my mother's and my father's side. The ancestry of my siblings, where it is known, is included in the chapters of each of their mothers.

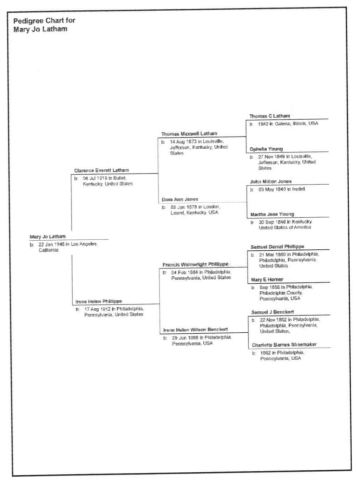

Pedigree Chart for Mary Jo Latham

Mary Jo Latham
b: 22 Jan 1946 in Los Angeles, California

Clarence Everett Latham
b: 04 Jul 1919 in Bullet, Kentucky, United States

Thomas Maxwell Latham
b: 14 Aug 1873 in Louisville, Jefferson, Kentucky, United States

Thomas C Latham
b: 1842 in Galena, Illinois, USA

Ophelia Young
b: 27 Nov 1849 in Louisville, Jefferson, Kentucky, United States

Dora Ann Jones
b: 03 Jan 1878 in London, Laurel, Kentucky, USA

John Milton Jones
b: 03 May 1840 in Iredell

Martha Jane Young
b: 30 Sep 1840 in Kentucky, United States of America

Irene Helen Phillippe
b: 17 Aug 1912 in Philadelphia, Pennsylvania, United States

Francis Wainwright Phillippe
b: 04 Feb 1884 in Philadelphia, Pennsylvania, United States

Samuel Daniel Phillippe
b: 21 Mar 1860 in Philadelphia, Philadelphia, Pennsylvania, United States

Mary E Horner
b: Sep 1858 in Philadelphia, Philadelphia County, Pennsylvania, USA

Irene Helen Wilson Benckert
b: 29 Jun 1888 in Philadelphia, Pennsylvania, USA

Samuel J Benckert
b: 22 Nov 1862 in Philadelphia, Philadelphia, Pennsylvania, United States

Charlotte Barnes Shoemaker
b: 1862 in Philadelphia, Pennsylvania, USA

Notes: Iredell is in North Carolina. The Joneses ended up in Kentucky. My mother's family were Philadelphians long before these generations.

About the Author

Mary Jo Martin, a member of the Houston Writer's Guild, is an award-winning writer who lives in the suburbs of Houston, Texas. Her short story, set in South Carolina, about domestic abuse and a poisoning, *Flowers for Lewis*, was published in a Houston Writer's Guild Press anthology, *Waves of Suspense* (2015). Another short story about scars, *The Life of Riley*, appeared in the online literary magazine, *Short Fiction Break*.

A personal medical mystery led her on a quest to find her father's medical history. Instead, she discovered a huge family. This work, *Sibling Revelries*, won first place in the memoir category in a Houston Writer's Guild contest, and an honorable mention in a Houston Writer's House contest.

Made in the USA
Columbia, SC
14 July 2019